monastic

staffordshire

Religious Houses in Medieval
Staffordshire and its Borderlands

John L. Tomkinson

CHURNET VALLEY BOOKS
Leek, Staffordshire. 01538 399033
email:picture.book@virgin.net web:freespace.virgin.net/c.hinton/

In Memoriam

Lily Tomkinson née Asher
V. Gordon Owen

Acknowledgements

My thanks are particularly due to Linda and Andrew Booker,
without whose help this book would not have been written.

contents

Acknowledgements
Introduction

The 13th century west wall of the Abbey Church, Croxden, showing the central west doorway and three lancet windows

Linda Owen

introduction

Between eight and five hundred years ago, life in Staffordshire was dominated by communities of monks, nuns and friars. They owned much of the land, organised agriculture, developed industries, engaged in commerce, and acted as leaders of society. Then, on the orders of King Henry VIII, within the space of three years, between 1536 and 1539, they vanished. Their buildings were deliberately destroyed, converted to other uses or simply allowed to deteriorate. Today there are few obvious reminders of the part they once played in creating our landscape and society, yet there are not many areas of the county where some trace of their existence and activities cannot be detected by research or a discerning eye.

This book is an attempt to place before the reader a brief outline of the origins, nature and development of these institutions, an assessment of the contribution they made to the development of our economy, the events surrounding their disappearance, and an indication of the traces which their activities have left behind.

In order to place the development of monasticism in Staffordshire in a historical context, Chapter One provides a brief survey of the history and characteristics of the area into which the first monks arrived, and of their earliest attempts at settlement before the Norman Conquest.

During the centuries which followed the end of the first millennium Europe saw a dramatic flowering of the monastic life. First there was a revival of traditional monasticism. Then groups of priests, or canons, came together to live under a quasi-monastic rule. A third wave of religious enthusiasm swept across Europe with the creation of stricter reformed orders, some of them combining religious with military duties. Finally, the thirteenth century saw the birth of the new orders of friars, actively engaged in the daily life of the townspeople. Chapters Two to Six consider each of these movements in turn, with a brief examination of some aspects of the history of the communities founded in our area during those years. Although ancient, the county boundaries are artificial lines, existing in our minds and records, rather than on the ground, and where it seemed appropriate I have included houses strictly lying outside the county, although close to its borders. The historical narrative ends in Chapter Seven with an account of the Dissolution of the Staffordshire religious houses.

Chapter Eight is a survey of the various sources of information from which their history may be recovered. In Chapter Nine I have expressed some general observations concerning the character of the Staffordshire foundations, and their contribution to the development of the region.

The spelling of extracts from late medieval documents originally written in English, often inconsistent even within a single document, has been standardised and modernised. The spelling of medieval surnames made up of the name of a place preceded by 'de' has been standardised where the place is readily identifiable. The French 'de' has been retained only where the place-name is Norman-French, 'of'

The Religious Houses of Medieval Staffordshire and its Borderlands

being substituted where it is English.

Wherever possible, I have avoided the technical language of medieval religion, architecture and law. Where periphrasis would render the text inconveniently verbose or repetitive, such terms as are unavoidable have been explained on their first appearance in the text. For the convenience of readers not following the text sequentially, definitions are provided in a glossary in Appendix One.

In a book of this size it is not possible to do much more than provide the reader with a small sample of the rich tapestry of the history of our religious houses. I would heartily recommend the reader who finds the subject interesting to follow up his reading by moving on to the much more detailed and scholarly works listed in the bibliography in Appendix Two. For the reader who is interested in visiting the sites of those religious houses which still have visible and accessible remains, I have included a gazetteer of information in Appendix Three.

An 18th century engraving entitled 'A Cistercian Abbey in Staffordshire'
based upon the ruins of Croxden Abbey..

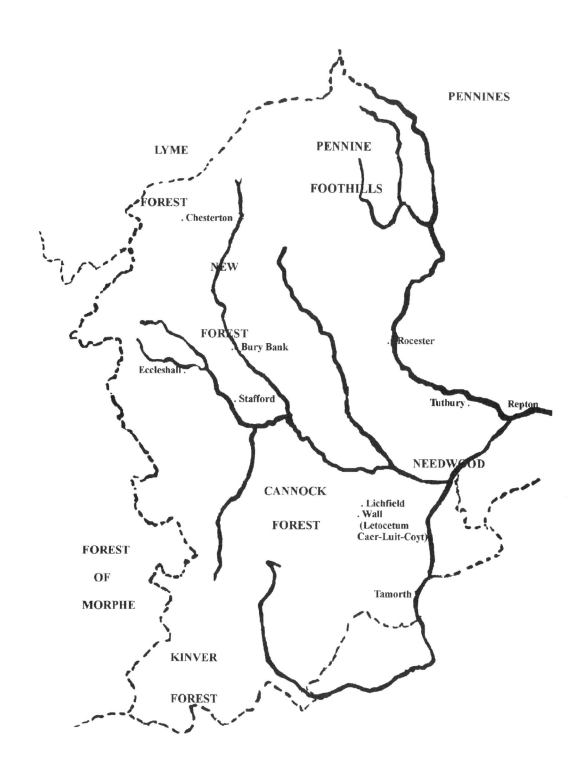

Early Staffordshire

chapter one
early and medieval staffordshire

The greater part of the English landscape was once clothed with woodlands, including much of the now bleak Pennine moorlands. Professor Ian Simmons of Durham University explains the disappearance of the high woodland as a result of human activity between the end of the last Ice Age and the beginning of settled farming (circa 10,000 - 4,500 BC). He argues that the woodland was deliberately burned to encourage the growth of plants favoured by the red deer, then hunted for its meat. This destruction was followed by permanent agricultural settlement in many places. Increased population density led to further small-scale clearance and widespread animal grazing, so that the Pennines was dotted with small villages by the beginning of the Christian era. The most obvious result of these developments was the demise of much of the high woodland and its replacement by the bleak open moorland so familiar to us today.

The Pennine foothills and the lower land throughout the rest of the county, however, would have remained covered in almost unbroken stretches of oak woods. Thus in the north lay the extensive woodland area of Lyme, the name of which is preserved in place-names such as Burslem, Newcastle-under-Lyme, and Audlem, while to the south lay the wooded areas later known as Needwood and Cannock. On all sides except the east, these wooded areas stretched into neighbouring counties: to the north in Cheshire lay the extensive wooded area of Mondrum, to the south Kinver and Arden, and to the west, Morphe in Shropshire.

Christianity first arrived in England during Roman times, but left little trace of its presence. It used to be thought that when, in 410, the Roman legions withdrew from Britain, Romano-British culture, society and economy collapsed almost immediately, leading to a return to Celtic tribalism. Certainly there was an immediate and marked decline in settlement in the Pennines, as marginal lands in the hill country were deserted and cultivation retreated to the river valleys. But recent evidence shows that while in some parts of Britain the Roman withdrawal did lead to a major crisis, in the west the survival of the Romano-British rural economy was prolonged into the late sixth or seventh century.

Roman Britain comprised some four or five provinces. Before AD 500, the Anglo-Saxon invasions had probably affected only two of these. Even by AD 600, most of what had been Roman Britain was still under the control of the descendants of inhabitants of the former Roman provinces. By this time, the Romano-British tribal areas had probably evolved into kingdoms. Wroxeter, in Shropshire, may have been the capital of one of these, for parts of the town were rebuilt after the fifth century with Romanised buildings, and these were occupied until the late sixth or even the early seventh century.

Christian monasticism originated in Egypt, when individuals retired into the desert to live alone (*monos*) with God. These 'Desert Fathers', the predecessors of the monks, at first lived as solitaries or hermits. Later, groups gathered into small communities and shared some aspects of their life together. Monasticism first appeared in Britain in the western, Romano-British areas of the country.

Mercia

For a variety of reasons, historians are increasingly coming to the view that rather than a large-scale invasion from the continent by the Angles and Saxons, only a small number of invaders actually settled in Britain. Rather than military conquest, changes in the balance of political and military power led to the disappearance of Romano-British ways and connections in favour of north European customs, religion and language. However, a number of invaders did establish themselves in positions of leadership over most of what came to be known as England. Anglians advancing inland from the East Coast during the mid-sixth century, following the valley of the River Trent, created the kingdom of Mercia by uniting or conquering the people of the Trent valley. Staffordshire and Derbyshire lay at the heart of this kingdom. Its early centres included Tamworth, Bury Bank, near Stone, and Repton, in Derbyshire.

Settlements during this period were confined to the valleys of the Trent and its tributaries, and it was only during the seventh century that a gradual reoccupation of the less attractive lands began. It was then, and in the centuries which immediately followed, that most of our villages were founded.

Mary Gelling has shown how village names may be used reveal the state of the landscape during this period. Names containing the elements *tun* and *leah* were used in areas which still retained considerable tree cover. As we should expect, place-names containing these elements are rare in the Pennines, since most of the high woodlands had already disappeared, but they are common in the Pennine foothills, in the rest of the county, and beyond its northern, western and southern borders. The element *tun* signified a settlement in what was already open country, while *leah* denoted a settlement made in a clearing within the woodland. Thus Repton, Wolverhampton and Longton were set up in what was then already open country, although thickly dotted with woods and copses, while Hanley, Audley and Dudley were originally clearings made within existing woodland.

The Coming of the Monks

In 597, Pope Gregory sent the monk Augustine, to Kent to convert the English. At the same time Celtic missionaries from Wales and Ireland arrived in the north of England. North and south of the kingdom of Mercia the people were converted to Christianity and communities of monks and nuns established. However, under the fiercely conservative King Penda, the by now powerful midland kingdom resisted this trend for some time. The names of pagan gods incorporated into place-names in Southern Staffordshire, such as Wednesbury (Woden's Bury), attest to the tenacity with which paganism resisted the return of Christianity in those parts.

It was only when Chad established his bishopric at Lichfield, between 669 and 672, that the conversion of Mercia began. Several religious communities were probably set up in this area during the years that followed, although little remains of most of them but legends.

According to a medieval story, when Chad converted Wulfad and Rufinus, two of the sons of King Wulfhere, their enraged father killed them. Later, when he had himself adopted Christianity, Wulfhere founded a monastery at Stone as a penance. Certainly, when Stone priory was founded in the mid-twelfth century, there was already a church in the town dedicated to Saint Wulfad which boasted his remains.

Unfortunately, there are problems with this colourful and entertaining story. Wulfhere, son of Penda, was already a Christian when he became king. Moreover, the same story appears in Bede's *Ecclesiastical History* - but set ten years later and in another part of the country. It is likely that this story was at some point 'borrowed' and adapted to account for veneration of the tomb of Wulfad in Stone Church.

Saint Werburgh, the daughter of King Wulfhere, became abbess of a convent at Hanbury and was buried there about the year 700. However, the story that she also founded a nunnery at Trentham is based upon a misinterpretation, made during the last century, of a document from Saint Werburgh's Abbey, Chester. This referred to the foundation of a convent by Werburgh at a place called 'Tricengeham', which has now been definitively identified with Threckingham in Lincolnshire.

There was also a medieval tradition that an Irish abbess, Saint Modwen, who died at about the same time, may have founded a monastery at Burton-on-Trent, but there is no hard evidence in support of this story.

Repton Abbey

The only monastic foundation of this period in our area about which we can be certain is that of Repton, in Derbyshire. A tradition says that St. David of Wales founded it in or about the year 600, although it seems highly unlikely that if that was so, it would have survived the reign of the fiercely conservative King Penda. A Celtic monastery, like most in that tradition it contained both men and women, but was always under the control of a woman. Alfthritha was abbess in 697, when it is recorded that St. Guthlac, repenting of the wild excesses of his youth, arrived at the monastery of Repton (already described as 'famous') to become a monk and do penance for his sins.

In the early eighth century two strong Mercian rulers, Aethelbold (716-757) and Offa (757-796) briefly established the dominance of Mercia over almost the whole of England. Offa, was the first to call himself 'king of the English'. There is some evidence that at that time a school of clerks was employed to copy manuscripts at Lichfield, which became for a short period, the seat of an archbishop. Today the most visible product of his reign is the earthwork known as Offa's Dyke: a ditch and bank twenty-five feet high, sixty feet wide and twice as long as Hadrian's Wall, built to protect the kingdom from the Welsh. After Offa's death, the Mercians lost their supremacy to the kings of Wessex, in the south, who came to be recognised as overlords of England.

Throughout this period, Repton Abbey was the chosen burial place of many of the Kings of Mercia, probably beginning with Aethelbold in 757. Their tombs lay in the crypt of the abbey church, now the parish church. When Wystan, grandson of King Wiglaf, was murdered in 849, he was buried in the mausoleum of his grandfather. It was said that a beam of light joined the place of his death with heaven, remaining visible for thirty days. He was thus regarded as a saint, and the presence of his shrine attracted pilgrims to Repton.

Linda Owen

Linda Owen

The crypt of the Parish Church of Repton, formerly the church of the Mercian Abbey.

Left: Entrance to the Anglo-Saxon crypt.

Right: Stairs cut into the fabric of the church to accommodate pilgrims to the shrine of St Wystan.

OPPOSITE PAGE: The Parish Church of Repton, formerly the church of the Mercian Abbey.
Top: The Anglo-Saxon chancel.
Bottom left: The mausoleum of King Wiglaf.
Bottom right: Site of the shrine of St Wystan.

Linda Owen

Linda Owen

Saint Benedict carrying his *Rule*, from the 15th century Breviary of Martin of Aragon, Spain.

Drawing of an Anglo-Saxon grave slab found near the site of Repton Abbey Church in 1801 and recorded in Lyson's *Magna Britannia*. By the middle of the century it had been broken up to use as a door-step.

Above: Saint Benedict writing the *Rule*.
A pen-drawing in a codex from the Benedictine and Imperial Abbey of Our Lady, Zwiefalten, Germany.

Saint Benedict

The Viking Invasions

After raiding the East Coast of England for many years, in 865 Danish Vikings began the systematic conquest of the country. In 867, they attacked Mercia, and in 873 occupied Repton. Monastic life there was brought to an abrupt end, but somehow the church and its shrine survived. The nuns of Hanbury fled to Chester with the remains of Saint Werburgh, although soon afterwards the Danes captured that city as well, establishing control over the whole of the north of England, which became known as the Danelaw.

King Alfred of Wessex, who placed himself at the head of all those resisting the invaders, made great efforts to preserve English culture, yet although he fostered scholars from Mercia, the Danish invasions seem to have totally destroyed monasticism in England.

During this period, Staffordshire found itself a contested border area. Alfred's son, Edward the Elder, who became King of Wessex in 899, began the reconquest of the Danelaw. His sister, Queen Aethelflaed of Mercia, set herself to recover the Five Danish boroughs of Derby, Nottingham, Leicester, Lincoln, and Stamford. Before she died, she had fortified Tamworth and Stafford, and captured Derby and Leicester. When Edward took Nottingham, all the Danes of Mercia submitted to him.

Unfortunately, he and his successor then had to deal with Vikings from Norway, who invaded the Wirral and the Lancashire coast from Ireland, crossing the Pennines and reaching York in 919. Thus it was not until the reign of King Edgar (959-975) that religious houses began to appear again in England, stimulated by a great archbishop of Canterbury, the Benedictine monk, St. Dunstan.

By this time most monasteries in Western Europe followed the *Rule* of St. Benedict, originally devised around 535-540 for his hilltop monastery of Monte Cassino, overlooking the road between Naples and Rome. Generally admired for the way in which it integrated prayer, manual labour and study into a well-rounded daily routine, it provided a complete blueprint for the administration of a monastery. The *Rule* laid down that each house was to be self-supporting, and that with few exceptions, each monk should spend the rest of his life in the monastery into which he had been admitted. The abbot of each house was to be elected for life by the monks, who were thereafter to live in complete obedience to him. Smaller communities, known as priories, were governed by a prior responsible to the abbot of their 'mother' house.

The Benedictine Rule was adopted throughout Western Europe, and the houses of black monks (known as such because of the colour of the habit, or robe, which they wore) became centres of learning during the Dark Ages. By the year 1066, there were some three dozen Benedictine houses in England. Two of these lay in Staffordshire.

The Founding of Burton Abbey

The abbey of Burton-on-Trent was founded, according to the monastery's own *Annals*, in 1004 by Wulfric Spot, a Saxon thegn, or nobleman, who owned extensive lands stretching from Yorkshire to Gloucestershire. The monks were drawn from the great abbey of Winchester, in the south of England; and for many years afterwards a monk of Winchester would always be appointed abbot of Burton-on-Trent.

During this century Viking raids resumed, and in 1010 Wulfric Spot died of wounds he had received during the battle of Ringmere. He was buried with his wife in the cloisters of the abbey he had founded. In his will, Wulfric left extensive lands to Burton Abbey on both sides of the border of the county with Derbyshire. Although some of the places listed cannot now be identified, those in Staffordshire included the manors of Burton, Stretton, Bromley, Gailey, Darlaston, Leigh, Okeover, Ilam, Calton and Rudyard. There were also extensive lands not merely in Derbyshire, but also in Shropshire, Leicestershire and Warwickshire. Wulfric left a large amount of livestock to the abbey, including one hundred wild horses and sixteen tame geldings. He also stipulated that a share of the fish obtained from his estates in the Wirral, Lancashire and Yorkshire should regularly be sent to the abbey. In his will, he asked the King to act as its patron, or guardian, after his death.

At the beginning of the eleventh century there was a second Danish invasion of England, and by 1017, the Danish King Cnut (Canute) had established control over the country. Since many of the estates listed in Wulfric Spot's will were no longer in the hands of the monastery after the Norman Conquest, they may have been lost during this invasion. Some of them, however, may have been swapped for others closer to the abbey site, since the lands later held by the abbey were all in Staffordshire and Derbyshire, and as such they would have been much more convenient to administer.

Burton Abbey was originally dedicated to St Benedict and All Saints, although it was later known as the abbey of St Mary and St Modwen, as the monks had come to believe that an earlier establishment, founded by the Irish Saint Modwen, had preceded their own before the first Danish invasion. Many monasteries derived profit from pilgrims attracted by miracle-working shrines. For example, after 'discovering' the graves of King Arthur and Queen Guinevere on their premises in 1191, the monks of Glastonbury never looked back. The supposed tomb of Saint Modwen at Burton was turned into a shrine, and her relics soon gained a reputation for working miracles, and so attracted pilgrims.

The Founding of Lapley Priory

In 1061 Burchard, the son of Earl Algar of Mercia and grandson of Lady Godiva of Coventry, was returning from a visit to Rome in company with Archbishop Aldred of York when he was taken seriously ill at Rheims, in France. Realising that he was dying, he asked to be buried in the monastery of St-Rémy, promising lands in England in payment.

His father duly provided lands at Lapley, Hamstall Ridware, Meaford, and Church Eaton in Staffordshire, and Silvington in Shropshire, enabling a small cell to be set up at Lapley, staffed by a small number of monks from St-Rémy. Their purpose was merely to manage the estates and export their profits to France; they did not live a full monastic life.

Lapley Parish Church, the former Priory Church.
Originally cruciform in shape, the transepts were
demolished, after the departure of the monks in 1414,
to reduce the size of the church.

The Norman Conquest

In 1066, King Harold was famously defeated by Duke William of Normandy at Hastings, after which the Conqueror advanced on London and was crowned King of England in Westminster Abbey. The English were very reluctant to accept his rule, and during the next few years there were constant rebellions. William ruthlessly stamped out opposition wherever it broke out.

In 1069 Edric the Wild and his Welsh allies occupied Shrewsbury and Chester as part of a general revolt throughout the West Country. William was forced to leave these rebels to their own devices for some time, as he had to deal with a more serious rising in Northumberland, which was supported by the Danish king. After capturing York, William devastated the north. Then, sending part of his army to intimidate the resentful inhabitants of the Fens, he crossed the Pennines with the rest of his forces to face the threat posed by Edric and the Welsh princes. By this time the rebels had gathered a formidable force, which included the men of Staffordshire and Cheshire. But as the Conqueror approached, Edric withdrew with his Herefordshire and Shropshire men, leaving the Welsh, together with the men of Staffordshire and Cheshire, to face the Normans at the battle of Stafford. After their defeat, William laid waste the surrounding area.

The Conqueror then made his way south-east, re-erecting castles the rebels had burned down, and re-garrisoning them. When he was ready, he turned back to deal with Chester, still defiantly holding out against him. In January 1070, William's army once more crossed the Pennines. This time the weather was bad, and the land offered them no sustenance, since they themselves had previously laid it waste. Suffering both from the weather and from sporadic attacks by local guerrilla fighters, mercenaries from the northern provinces of France mutinied. When the Conqueror abandoned them in the hills and advanced on Chester with his more resilient Normans, the city submitted without resistance.

By 1073, William was secure in his dominance of England. Castles had been erected and garrisoned at Stafford, Tutbury, Shrewsbury, Warwick, Worcester and many other places. Against his more usual practice, in the Marches, or border areas, William gave to specially trusted followers lands concentrated in a single region, in order that they should be able to maintain the strength necessary to resist any further revolt. Roger of Montgomery controlled Shropshire. Hugh d'Avranches, 'the Wolf', was given extensive powers as Earl of Chester. Henry de Ferrers received over one hundred manors in Derbyshire, although his chief seat was the castle of Tutbury.

These events must have considerably set back the development of Staffordshire and its neighbouring counties. The Domesday Book of 1086, a detailed survey of England, records a large number of Staffordshire manors as 'waste'. Many others are described as having fewer working ploughs than would have been required to service the available arable land - clear evidence of systematic depopulation.

A further brake on the development of much of this region was the imposition of forest law on vast tracts of land. In addition to the creation of the royal forest of Cannock, an area stretching from the north of Stoke-on-Trent southwards to Tixall was placed under forest administration as the 'New Forest' of Staffordshire.

Linda Owen

Tutbury castle on its hill. Norman power dominating an English countryside.

The term 'Forest' was a legal term applied to land where only the monarch could hunt, which was subject to special laws against poaching, designed for the protection of deer. In some parts of the country entire villages were destroyed and their inhabitants driven out when the forests were created. John of Worcester charged that the Conqueror had depopulated a fruitful and prosperous countryside to make way for deer, and in popular myth the death of his successor, William Rufus, while hunting in the New Forest, was an act of divine retribution. But modern research suggests that the Norman kings imposed forest laws mainly upon districts where clearing and cultivation had previously made only slow progress, or in areas of agriculturally unfavourable land.

At this time Staffordshire was an underdeveloped area. The bears and beavers had probably disappeared before the first Danish invasion, but wolves, wild boar and wild horses were still found. Settlements were generally small, poor and pastoral. Cattle and swine were reared across the county, with horses in Needwood, Cannock and Kinver, and sheep in the north and east. Oats was the chief grain crop, bread being made from oats and rye, rather than wheat, (the practice in the Pennine area until the eighteenth century). It may be that the development of Staffordshire had been slowed down during the period when it had been a contested border area with the Danelaw, and it was always liable to raids by marauding Welshmen. The Conqueror had brought a hostile army into the area, defeated its inhabitants in battle, and then laid waste the surrounding region. In the next year he had abandoned a mutinous force in the Pennines. Each of these campaigns must have had a devastating effect on the countryside. Certainly the Norman armies had wrought considerable destruction, and the subsequent application of forest laws would have impeded further development.

Following the Conquest, in political terms Staffordshire was once again a border area. The north of the county lay adjacent to the virtually independent County Palatine of Chester, where the most important matters were settled by the earls and their agents without reference to royal authority. The south was dominated by the earls of Derby who held their court at Tutbury. The most notable lords whose main estates lay within the county were the considerably less important barons of Stafford, descended from Robert, the younger son of Ralph de Toeni, hereditary standard bearer of the Normans.

chapter two
the black monks and nuns

Burton Abbey

The seal of the Abbey of Burton.

Despite his military ferocity, the Conqueror went out of his way to secure the loyalty of the monks of Burton. When he learned that they had received Coton-in-the-Elms, in Derbyshire as a gift from the rebel earl Morkar, he promptly seized it from them. But he returned it when he made a personal visit as a pilgrim to the shrine of Saint Modwen, at the same time adding further lands and property in Derbyshire. Unusually, the English abbot, Leofric, was not replaced by a Norman; and Englishmen continued to be appointed as abbots of Burton for another fifty years. This monastery actually benefited from the Norman Conquest.

Parish churches were major sources of income for monasteries, since religious taxes of one tenth of their annual produce, called tithes, were levied on the peasants to pay for their upkeep, to support the priests who served them and to provide alms for the poor. The monasteries would sometimes act as patrons of a church, receiving an annual payment from its funds, usually the third set aside for the poor, since they had supposedly made themselves poor 'for the sake of Christ'. However, they might sometimes acquire the right to appropriate the entire income of the church for their own use, and pay a vicar to manage the parish on their behalf. Parish churches and their dependent chapels which came under the control of Burton Abbey, in addition to that of Burton-on-Trent itself, included Mickleover, Bromley, Leigh, Stapenhill, Willington, Austrey and Ilam.

Among other properties acquired were houses in Derby and a house in London, left to the abbey in the will of a fishmonger. By the 1320s a moated house had been built outside Burton, called Sinai Park, which was used as a convalescent home and sanatorium for aged or sick monks. It was also used for the regular blood-letting, using live leeches, which was insisted upon for all monks by the *Rule* as a health precaution.

The townspeople of Burton undoubtedly profited from the proximity of the

Linda Owen

Linda Owen

Linda Owen

Sinai House. The Monks' convalescent home, extensively rebuilt during the early 16th century.

abbey. At the end of the twelfth century the abbot secured royal permission to make the town a borough, and to hold a weekly market and an annual fair. Similar rights were secured for Abbots Bromley a few years later. Archaeological evidence suggests that the town was rebuilt, or extensively developed, by the abbey during the late thirteenth century, the buildings being laid out systematically in a grid pattern. During the fifteenth century, the abbey provided the town with a grammar school, a market hall, and a piped water supply.

The abbots of Burton became important leaders of society in the county, having the right to hold court, appoint a coroner, erect gallows and inflict the death penalty. From time to time the abbot was summoned to Parliament, where he would take his seat among the 'Lords Spiritual' of the realm.

The main business of the abbey was the management of its estates. Granges, or outlying farmsteads, were established at Burton, Shobnall, Stapenhill, Stretton, Winshill and Branston, in Staffordshire, and at Newton, Hunsden and Findern in Derbyshire.

By the late thirteenth century, the abbey kept sheep. A fulling mill for the manufacture of cloth from wool was erected in Burton during the 1340s. When beaten and purified with fullers' earth, the woven cloth would shrink until its texture became almost invisible, and the finished material more resistant to wear and tear. Small hammers moved by water power performed this process mechanically. The erection of a fulling mill involved considerable financial investment, and would have required the employment of a large number of weavers in the town to make it financially worthwhile.

During the 1190s, Burton Abbey obtained a salt pit and salt pan at Nantwich. Salt was not only needed for the preservation of meat, but also for butter and cheese. Salt also had a multitude of other uses, from the manufacture of medicines to the soldering of pipes and gutters. It was usually obtained from salters travelling the 'saltways', but the abbeys preferred to collect it from one of the 'wiches' or salt towns once a year. During the early thirteenth century, the abbey was also working its own quarry, probably at Winshill.

In common with a pattern repeated across England, by the fourteenth century most of the abbey estates, including its granges and other assets, were no longer worked or managed by the monks themselves, but were leased out to laymen in return for money rents.

The miracle-working remains of Saint Modwen attracted significant numbers of pilgrims from the surrounding countryside. Most of the alleged miracles worked there seem to have been healings from blindness and disease. For example, a young man named Godric, while joking with some girls, inadvertently swallowed a pin. He fasted, prayed, and then took a snack in the abbey kitchen. Shortly afterwards, he vomited up the food, some blood and the offending pin. Like all medieval saints, St Modwen could be vindictive as well as benign. It is recorded that a goldsmith who stole from her shrine accidentally fell upon his own spear and was painfully and fatally disembowelled.

Because it was under royal patronage, several kings of England stayed at Burton Abbey, where a room was known as the 'King's Chamber'. Henry II visited in 1155, while King John, Henry III and Edward I each visited on several occasions. These were not mere courtesy calls. Travelling about the country with their court was the way in which the kings of England supported themselves and maintained their authority. They would consume the resources of their own manors and enjoy the hospitality of those who, like the monks of Burton, benefited from their protection.

Not all royal visits were routine, however. During a revolt by Thomas, Earl of Lancaster, Lord of Tutbury, against Edward II in 1322, the rebels occupied Burton Bridge in an attempt to prevent the King from crossing the Trent. This proved ineffective, since the royal forces forded the river upstream. Although the rebels burned the town before they retreated, there is some evidence that abbot Sudbury of Burton may have supported them, since he was later accused of allowing earl Thomas to store his money in the abbey.

Despite its generous endowments, Burton Abbey suffered continually from financial problems. These seem to have been due either to incompetent administration or to the attentions of predatory patrons and neighbours - mostly the former.

In 1094, Abbot Geoffrey Mauland, and in 1159 Abbot Robert, were each deposed for 'dissipating the lands and goods of the abbey'. Any monk who was elected abbot seemed to consider what use he could make of abbey lands in the support of his family and friends. In 1319 at the request of the community a royal clerk was temporarily installed to sort out the debts of the abbey and oversee its administration. In 1382 the monks were allowed to appropriate the income of Austrey Church for ten years because the abbey was 'so impoverished through dearness of corn and mortality of cattle, and lawsuits which it had been obliged to undergo, that the monks can no longer maintain hospitality or even live decently'. In 1384 it was placed under royal protection 'on account of its oppression by rivals and the consequent diminution of divine service and works of charity'. In 1400, the king pardoned all the abbey's debts because it had been impoverished by the 'improvident governance' of the recently deposed abbot. The same thing happened in 1414 because of its 'notable dilapidation' due to 'the bad governance of its abbots'. Debts had accumulated, and many of its possessions had been improvidently leased on disadvantageous terms. In 1422, as far as could be ascertained, debts totalled one hundred pounds, yet Abbot Sudbury was selling off the goods of the house and supporting his relatives at the community's expense. In 1424, Burton was once more placed under the administration of Royal Commissioners, and it is probably significant that later in that year abbot Sudbury resigned.

Yet the financial problems continued, and in 1433 a commission of laymen led by Earl Humphrey of Stafford was appointed to supervise the affairs of the abbey for seven years. Abbot Henley was suspended in 1454 for alienating monastic property and general extravagance. New privileges were granted to the house in 1468 'in consideration of the intolerable things which the abbey daily sustains'. After all that,

Linda Owen

Linda Owen

The Abbey Inn, Burton on Trent, originally the monastery infirmary.

Linda Owen

Linda Owen

Linda Owen

Linda Owen

Medieval beams and stonework in the
Abbey Inn and its grounds.

in 1498 the abbot and his officials were still not keeping proper accounts.

One practice which led to recurring financial problems was that of granting corrodies. A layman would give land or a sum of money to a monastery, and in return, the monks would guarantee him board and lodging of a specified standard in apartments within the monastery sometimes, with his own servants in attendance, for the rest of his life. This form of retirement pension was a gamble for both parties. If the corrodian died soon after the agreement, the abbey made a profit; if he lived for a long time afterwards, the corrodian had made a good investment. This practice was to become general throughout the country, but it seems to have originated at Burton-on-Trent.

Kings later took advantage of this practice to 'reward' servants and officials at no cost to themselves by insisting that an abbey of which they were patron grant them a corrody. Thus in 1310 Edward II ordered the monks of Burton to provide Sir Thomas of Banbury with a room inside the abbey precincts and food and clothing for life in return for his long service to the Crown. The monks pleaded poverty, but the king found their response 'frivolous, untruthful and unacceptable', and threatened to confiscate their lands. In 1316, when the king retired ageing members of his garrison at Berwick-on-Tweed, Nicholas of Derby was foisted on Burton Abbey for the rest of his life. From this point onwards, there was probably never a time when a retired royal official of some kind was not enjoying free maintenance at Burton.

In addition to this problem, the neighbouring gentry were sometimes in the habit of extracting 'protection money'. Abbot Southam paid thirty shillings a year to Sir John Bagot so that he would 'be a friend of the house'. In 1402, Abbot Sudbury complained that Bagot had robbed his park in Abbots Bromley to convince him that a more substantial payment was appropriate.

The bishops performed regular inspections of the monasteries in their dioceses, called 'visitations'. The surviving records of these reveal the internal problems of the community, and show that Burton Abbey was no more noted for rigorous observance of the monastic rule than it was for good bookkeeping.

In 1407, a royal pardon was necessary for acts of violence, 'ravishings' and thefts committed during the previous few years. Abbot Sudbury, who stands out in a succession of bad abbots, spent most of his Sundays with women, and was found guilty of adultery with two. He had, for example, on Christmas Day 1404 'in his chamber at Burton, ravished Margery, the wife of Nicholas Taverner'. Many of the monks regularly missed religious services since they were drinking in the town with their friends, as was the abbot himself. Two women of ill-repute actually lodged inside the walls of the monastery, while horses, dogs and hawks were kept for hunting. By 1414 the performance of divine worship had lapsed altogether. In 1422 the visitors complained that Abbot Sudbury did not sleep in the dormitory or eat in the refectory with the other monks, but maintained his own apartments, with a separate kitchen. He did not bother to hold regular chapter meetings.

In 1455 Abbot Henley was forced to resign because of his habitual absence from religious services, as well as for his gambling and drunkenness. During the 1460s a whore from Lichfield paid regular visits to the monastery, where 'she admitted the monks to carnal copulation'. In 1498 the Bishop instructed the Abbot to have the locks changed on the abbey gates, to see that they were closed at the proper times, to prevent access by women, and to bring an end to the monks' 'frequenting of taverns and other suspect places'.

Visitations early in the sixteenth century, just before the monasteries were closed down, show that, ironically, conditions had by that time improved considerably. In 1530 the sub-prior was on the waiting list for admission to the very strict Carthusian monastery of Mount Grace, in Yorkshire. In 1533 Abbot Bronston was chosen to be Abbot of Westminster, the highest position ever achieved by any monk from Staffordshire.

There were usually between fifteen and thirty fully professed monks at Burton at any one time. There were thirty-one in 1295, but this had gone down to fifteen in 1377. The fall in numbers over this period is common to most religious houses, and was due to the effects of the epidemic of 1349, known as the Black Death. In 1518, there were seventeen monks and three novices, making Burton Abbey the largest monastery in the area we are covering. It had an income double that of Tutbury and Dieulacres. Yet by the normal standards of English Benedictine houses, it was a small monastery.

The history of Burton Abbey illustrates the main failing of the Benedictine monasteries. Each abbey was an autonomous unit in which the monks were sworn to obey the abbot, but there was no one to exercise control over the abbot. Whether a monastery observed high standards or became a byword for corruption depended very largely upon the personality of the abbot, and from the likes of Abbots Sudbury and Henley little could be expected.

In medieval books, monks were frequently protrayed realistically. This could well be a monk of Burton, possibly even Abbot Sudbury himself.

Fabric of the medieval infirmary incorporated into the Abbey Inn.

Early 16th century fireplace in the cellars of the inn.

Linda Owen

Linda Owen

Stonework in the grounds of the Abbey Inn.

Linda Owen

Linda Owen

Burton Abbey Inn and its grounds.

Linda Owen

Linda Owen

Lapley Priory

Soon after the Norman Conquest, adventurers who had come to England with the Conqueror gave newly acquired lands to the religious houses they had left behind across the Channel. The Norman monasteries usually established small cells on their English lands, staffed by one or two monks under a prior, who acted as estate managers so as to allow the mother house to exploit the revenues of its new lands. This was generally considered preferable to setting up a fully-fledged daughter house, which would itself consume much of this income, and which might prove difficult to control. The new monasteries were thus a form of ecclesiastical colonialism. A Norman house was in existence at Lapley before the Conquest, and afterwards another was set up at Tutbury.

In 1086 there were just two French monks at Lapley. When, in later centuries, relations between the English and French had broken down, the presence of foreign monks became a cause of friction. When Normandy was lost to King John in 1204, he seized Lapley Priory and then returned it to the monks on payment of a fine. This convenient way of raising money was enthusiastically adopted by his successors. Lapley was seized in 1288 because the prior had travelled to Normandy without royal permission, and once more in 1325.

During the 1330s there was a dispute over which of the monks, Baldwin de Spynale or Gobert de Lapion, was properly the prior. Baldwin was in possession of the premises, but in an attack in 1335, Gobert and his allies removed 40 oxen, 15 bullocks, 15 heifers, and 40 pigs. The raiders, who included among their number the vicar of Lapley, also cut down trees, broke open chests and stole the priory deeds.

During the long period of war between France and England known as the Hundred Years War, those houses which sent substantial proportions of their income to mother houses abroad were officially designated 'alien priories'. They were taken into the King's hands, and forced to accept their lands as a gift from him - for a price, of course - promising not to act treasonably, nor to leave the country without permission, nor to export precious metals. Lapley was seized and placed under Gobert's control, but he was probably a victim of the Black Death, for Baldwin soon returned as prior. In 1354, he was complaining that the priory was impoverished as a result of the plague and a fire which had burned down most of the buildings.

In 1378 there was a general expulsion of foreign monks from the alien houses. They were ordered to leave the country through Dover, where they could be searched. The men of Lapley were exempted from this ruling, but in 1384 the priory was granted to the King's squire, Robert of Hampton, for the duration of the war, free of rent. On several other occasions subsequently the priory was given to various people to enjoy the income, while the annual payment due to the King was increased.

In 1414 the entire estate was handed over by the King to Tong College in Shropshire. Presumably the single remaining monk returned to France with relief.

OPPOSITE PAGE: Lapley Priory

Top: The Sedilia, or Seats for the Sacred Ministers, in the sanctuary.
Middle: Traces of medieval wall painting on the north wall.
Bottom: Remains of ancient arches which may originally have given access to chantry chapels.

Linda Owen

Linda Owen

Linda Owen

Lapley Priory
Top: Doorway giving access to the chancel. The small window is part of the original Norman building.

Bottom:
Tomb of a priest wearing Mass vestments. The inscription is very worn, but the name John is just visible. It is believed to be the tomb of John of Darlaston, Prior and Vicar of Lapley.

Linda Owen

Linda Owen

OPPOSITE PAGE:

Top left: The Piscina, a shelf and sink used for cleaning the sacred vessels during mass.

Bottom left: The Dutch Font. Scenes from the life of Christ carved around the bowl show it to be of 11th-12th century Dutch origin, with an inscription in Dutch added at some later date. No one knows how it found its way to Lapley, but a hypothetical Dutch monk has been suggested.

Top right: Looking towards the chancel, showing the massive Norman arch, an original feature of the church under the central tower, and the serious misalignment of the east end of the church with the west. This surprising feature of many medieval churches, including Lichfield Cathedral, is sometimes attributed to the builder's desire to represent the inclination of Christ's head as traditionally represented by crucifixes; but it may have had a much more mundane explanation.

Bottom right: The east wall and window of the church dating from the early 13th century.

Tutbury Priory

The second alien house in Staffordshire, the priory of Tutbury, was founded in 1080 by Henry de Ferrers. Ostensibly it was in memory of William the Conqueror and his wife, Matilda of Flanders, but the monks were drawn from the Norman abbey of Saint-Pierre-sur-Dives in a clear attempt to increase Norman influence in South Staffordshire. The community was originally granted lands in Tutbury and Rolleston, and the churches of Tutbury Castle and Mayfield. Henry's wife, Bertha, also gave to them Stanford-in-the-Vale, in Berkshire, which was exchanged for Church Broughton, Norbury and Edlaston in Derbyshire. The founder and his wife were buried in the priory church which, unusually, also served as parish church. Lands were later acquired in Derbyshire, including Marston-on-Dove, Doveridge, and West Broughton and the church of Norbury.

Unlike Lapley, Tutbury was a conventual priory in which a group of Norman monks led a full monastic life. It functioned as an almost independent community, although a sum of money had to be sent each year to the mother house. The prior had to report to Saint-Pierre on the condition of the community every three years, and the father abbot had the right to appoint or depose the prior. By the mid-thirteenth century the abbot would nominate three candidates for the post, and then the patron would choose one of them.

The monks sometimes suffered at the hands of their own 'guardians' or patrons. Robert, Earl Ferrers, destroyed the priory buildings when he came of age in 1260. The monks took him to court, and by 1263 he had agreed not to interfere with their rights any more in return for their dropping legal proceedings against him. When Robert found himself on the losing side in the Barons' Wars in 1266, all his possessions were forfeit. The castle and estates, including the patronage of Tutbury Priory, were transferred to Edmund, Earl of Lancaster.

Inevitably, with the outbreak of the Hundred Years War with France, this community, like that at Lapley, found itself the focus of considerable hostility. The king ordered an assessment of its wealth, and then seized the priory, restoring ownership to the monks in return for an annual payment of thirty pounds. The officials of their own patron, Earl Thomas, terrorised the priory and damaged its estates. In a move to anglicise the monastery, in 1308 a monk of Burton-on-Trent was appointed prior by the bishop.

In 1322 Earl Thomas rebelled against Edward II, was defeated and executed. Shortly after he had abandoned Tutbury Castle, and before the King had arrived, a large amount of money, jewellery and goods was removed and stored in the priory. This included £1,500 in cash and seven cartloads of silver and other ornaments, including cloth of gold worth £300. The officials claimed that it had been moved only to ensure its security, and this was accepted. However, a further £40 worth of goods and a barrel of sturgeon were later found in the possession of Prior Robert of Longdon, which he claimed were gifts from the King. The court demanded that he obtain the King's confirmation of his story, which he was unable to do, and he was fined £70.

Tutbury Parish Church, formerly the Priory Church. After the dissolution, the church was demolished save for the nave. The French-style semi-circular chancel is a modern addition.

This was a bad time for Prior Robert. He was excommunicated, formally cast out of the Church and cursed, in that same year, for failing to pay a pension due to the Dean and Chapter of Lichfield from the church of Mayfield, and the community was robbed of goods worth £80. In 1325 he acknowledged that, among other debts, he owed £100 to a Florentine merchant. He had probably been selling the annual wool crop of the abbey in advance of its production, a common practice which led many monasteries into debt during years when the crop was poorer than expected. Climate changes at this time had led to poor harvests and widespread outbreaks of livestock disease.

By this date there was an English majority among the monks, and the war with France divided the community itself. In 1329 Prior Robert left to become abbot of Burton-on-Trent, and English majority elected Giles of Longford to replace him. Earl Henry would not appoint him, preferring John of St-Aubyn, a monk of Saint-Pierre. The English monks refused to accept a Frenchman, and forced him to resign in 1335. They then elected one of their own number, Ralph of Coventry. Meanwhile, the abbot of Saint-Pierre presented three candidates to Earl Henry, from whom he chose Alexander de Portu. As soon as he arrived, the French nominee was kidnapped, presumably by the English monks or their friends, but released when the court confirmed the Earl's right to make the appointment. Unwilling to accept defeat, the English monks, headed by the sub-prior, Ralph of Derby, appealed to Pope Clement V and then the King, but in vain.

In 1337 the war with France was renewed, and the priory was seized by the King, and 'leased' to the Prior for an annual sum of one hundred marks. On the conclusion of peace in 1361 its independence was restored, but when the war recommenced in 1369 it was again seized. Not surprisingly, the community became increasingly impoverished.

When all the non-conventual houses were closed down in 1402, the prior had to prove that Tutbury was a conventual priory, that the monks there lived a full religious life and were not mere estate managers, like those at Lapley. Two men who wished to acquire the estate for themselves testified that it was not, and were believed. The priory was promptly seized, but when the truth was established, two years later, its independence was restored.

In 1410 royal permission was given for six French monks to be brought from Saint-Pierre, but in 1413 Parliament passed a law forcing the alien priories to admit only English monks in the future. In 1433, when the last French prior died, the monastery had become thoroughly anglicised.

Evidence of the later integration of the priory into the life of the local community is provided by the part played by the prior in providing a bull for the annual August bull run. This was probably instituted in or after 1371, when John of Gaunt, who held Tutbury Castle, married a Spanish princess, Constanza, and became king of Castille, in central Spain. It first appears in the records in 1414. The prior would provide a bull which would be covered with soap, maimed by cutting off its horns, ears and tail, and then further annoyed by having pepper blown up its nose. Then it would be baited by members of a 'court of minstrels' Gaunt had set up. The man who first cut off part of its bristles received the beast as his prize. This had to be done while the animal was still within the county boundary, which lay nearby. The practice survived the closure of the priory, and was continued until 1778.

Local traditions associate Tutbury and its priory with Robin Hood, and portray him as participating in the bull-baiting just before his wedding. One story has him married by the prior of Tutbury under a yew tree at Doveridge. The historical background to these romances is very confused, since the stories of Robin Hood are set during the reign of King Richard I, who preceded the bull-run by some two hundred years.

Tutbury Parish Church, formerly the Priory Church. The Great West Door.

Above: Alabaster carving on the West Door, the oldest of its kind in England.

Below: Norman doorways.

Linda Owen

Tutbury Church

Left: The West Front.

Right: Lancet window.

Linda Owen

Linda Owen

Linda Owen

Tutbury Church

Above: The Norman Interior:
The north-west of the nave.

Left: The Norman interior of
the West Front.

Deatails of alabaster carving on the West Door, Tutbury Church.

The Stocks, Tutbury.

Linda Owen

Linda Owen

Linda Owen

Linda Owen

Canwell Priory

This small priory, dedicated to Saint Giles, was probably founded about 1140 by Geva, an illegitimate daughter of Earl Hugh I of Chester. She donated some lands in Canwell, a house and lands at Drayton Basset and Dunton Basset, in Leicestershire, and the churches of Dunton Basset and Ragdale, also in Leicestershire. Later grants included a mill in Tamworth and lands in Sutton Coldfield, in Warwickshire. The Draytons of Bassett were patrons of the house until 1390 when the line became extinct. The earls of Warwick exercised patronage until the Lisle family took over the responsibility.

The endowment was not a large one, and it is likely that this community was always very small. During the fifteenth century there were usually only two or three monks in residence. In 1453 there was only one other member of the community in addition to Prior Sadeler, and he was living outside the priory and drawing a pension. When the prior died, three years later, the pensioner was ordered back into the monastery, and his pension spent on repairs to the church. From that time onwards, on the death of a prior, the bishop would appoint a successor from another monastery, since there were usually no other monks at all.

Considering how tiny this community was, it is surprising that its members may have included no less than two murderers. In 1272, the monk William of Sutton fled after being accused of homicide. He was outlawed, and the prior was fined one mark (13s 4d) for allowing him to escape. A later prior, John Bredon (1443-7), was himself imprisoned for murder, but subsequently pardoned.

Sandwell Priory

A hermitage by a spring in West Bromwich was chosen as the site of another very small monastery dedicated to St. Mary Magdalen by William de Offeni, a tenant of Gervase Paynel, Lord of Dudley, around 1190. The grant included land in West Bromwich and a half share in the rectory of Ellesborough, in Buckinghamshire. The patrons were the lords of West Bromwich, and the priory later acquired the parish church.

During the thirteenth century this community became involved in a protracted vendetta with the de Parles family. It probably began in 1211 when William de Parles unsuccessfully contested in the courts the abbey's right to lands in Sandwell and Handsworth. It continued when, twelve years later, John de Parles successfully disputed the priory's rights over Handsworth Church. It climaxed in 1260, when William de Parles led an armed band against the priory, and the prior was considered lucky to escape with his life.

This was another tiny community. When the prior died in the plague year, 1349, there was only one other monk left. The community never entirely recovered, although numbers increased slightly during the fifteenth century.

During the 1370s there was a dispute between John of Kyngeston and Richard Tudenham about which of them should be prior, with the result that John was shot in the arm with an arrow. The abbot of Shrewsbury seems to have tried to take control of the situation, although the method he used seems lacking in subtlety. In 1379, he and two other monks from Shrewsbury kidnapped John and took him to Sleap, one of the abbot's manors in Shropshire, where they made him renounce his claim. Then one of the monks involved in the kidnapping, Richard of Westbury, was installed as prior. This was resented by the other resident monk at Sandwell, Richard Tudenham, who considered that his own claim had been unjustly overlooked. He tried to bring the matter up in court, but was himself arrested for his pains.

In 1391 the bishop appointed John of Tamworth, a monk of Coventry, as prior. Six years later, he was temporarily forced out by a monk who had left the monastery, Alexander Leddersham, with the aid of an armed band of his friends. The next few appointments were all of monks from Shrewsbury, which seems to indicate that the Abbey was able to gain effective control of Sandwell for some time. Their oversight did not improve matters much, however, for in 1414 prior Richard Dudley was accused of sheltering murderers and robbers.

These struggles were attempts to gain control over the income from the priory endowments. Although not large, they would have provided a good living for the tiny number of people in residence. Alternatively, the abbots of Shrewsbury may have desired to use some of the income of Sandwell to supplement the endowments of their own house.

Brewood (Black Ladies) Priory

The proportion of men to women living the religious life in England during the Middle Ages has been estimated at about ten to one. Communities of women were not only less common than those of men, they were generally smaller and of less importance. Consequently, there is usually less information about them in the records. There were several nunneries in and near Staffordshire.

Linda Owen

Blackladies' Hall.

Linda Owen

Linda Owen

Left: Blackladies' Hall detail.

Above: Ancient door.

Bottom:
Late 15th or early 16th century panelling.

Linda Owen

Linda Owen

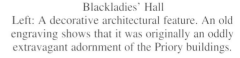

Blackladies' Hall
Left: A decorative architectural feature. An old
engraving shows that it was originally an oddly
extravagant adornment of the Priory buildings.

Below: The Priory fishpond.

Bottom left:
Medieval floor tiles excavated from the site of
the Priory Church.

Bottom right:
Probably the original beams of the Priory, re-used
in situ when the roof was raised.

Linda Owen

Linda Owen

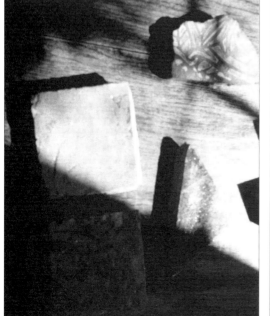

Linda Owen

St. Mary's Priory, the first of these, was located about two and a half miles west of the village of Brewood. A small community, its origins are obscure, although it was in existence by the mid-twelfth century. J. L. Kirby thought that it may have been founded by Bishop Roger de Clinton (1129-48), since it was situated on a manor of the bishops of Lichfield.

The nuns held lands and rents in Brewood, Blithbury, Bradley, Stretton; in Broom, Kidderminster and Halesowen in Worcestershire; and Tong in Salop.

An incident in 1276 illustrates the problems faced by anyone living in or near the forest. A stag drowned in the priory fish-pond. Instead of handing it over to the forest authorities as the law required, the nuns decided to try some venison, and shared the carcass with John Giffard of Chillington. Both parties were convicted of this serious offence against the forest laws, but whereas Giffard was fined and imprisoned, the nuns escaped with a royal pardon 'on account of their poverty'.

When Bishop Northburgh inspected the priory in 1323, he found much to complain about. We can infer what was wrong from the instructions for change he left behind. The prioress was ordered to eat in the refectory and sleep in the dormitory. Outsiders were not to reside in the priory, and in particular, 'the prioress's girl' was to be expelled. The nuns were not to go out without permission, or to converse with others outside. The income from a rent enjoyed by one of the nuns was in future to be used for the benefit of the whole community, and not the nun herself.

Blithbury Priory

At some time between 1129 and 1148 a house for two monks and a number of nuns was established on the south bank of the Blythe at Blithbury by Hugh de Ridware. Within a few years only nuns remained in residence. During the mid twelfth-century an unusually close association developed between this convent and the nuns of St. Mary's Brewood. By the fourteenth century, the two communities had merged, the community at Blithbury being assimilated into that at Brewood, its lands at Blithbury and Gailey augmenting the estates of Brewood Priory.

Farewell Priory

At some point Roger de Clinton (1129-48) gave to some hermits at Farewell in Cannock Forest, just two and a half miles north-west of Lichfield, some land they had already cleared there, and as much woodland as they could clear in the future. Around 1140 some nuns also took up residence there, and were given St. Mary's Church, a mill, wood, the cleared lands and six serfs. Hugh, the bishop's chaplain, gave them land which he had cleared from the woods at Pipe.

By the mid-twelfth century the community consisted exclusively of women. By the fourteenth century, this well-endowed nunnery was managing land at Farewell, Curborough and Hammerwich, keeping sheep, and receiving rents from estates at Chorley Abnalls, Ashmore Brook, Elmhurst, Longdon, and Hammerwich, and had a house in Lichfield.

When Bishop Roger Northburgh conducted a visitation of this prosperous house in 1331 he found the nuns wearing silk and sleeping two to a bed with young girls. He ordered them to put on their religious habits again, and forbade women over the age of twelve other than nuns from living in the house. Two live-in servants, Agnes of Lichfield and Margaret of Chorley, were dismissed, and the nuns told in future to employ only women of good reputation and conversation. The back door leading to the garden was to be kept locked in order to avoid certain (unspecified) scandals which had occurred in the past. Two nuns who had broken their vows were named. One, Alice of Kynynton, was to be disciplined; while an older and reliable nun was to keep her eye on Cecily of Gretton. The instructions left for the nuns had to be written in French because they could not read Latin well enough. This is evidence not only of lack of learning, but also of the nuns' social class. This was a convent for daughters of the gentry.

In 1367, Bishop Robert Stretton found things in a better state, although he found it necessary to order that the nuns were to keep only one child each to be educated in the priory, and that this must not include boys over the age of seven. Again it was ordered that ordinary women who were not priory servants were not to be allowed to live in. Nuns were not to go into Lichfield without the permission of the prioress, and then only in threes; and they were not to hang around in the town. They were not keeping accounts, and were to do so in the future. They were also to eat all their meals in common, and have no more fires except in the infirmary and guest hall.

The chancel of Farewell Parish Church, originally part of the Priory Church.

Repton Priory, looking across the site of the cloisters.

Repton Priory, part of the undercroft of the Refectory.

chapter three
the black canons

During the mid-eleventh century, great attempts were made, known as the Gregorian Reforms, to raise the standards of behaviour of the clergy and enforce clerical celibacy. The Lateran Synods of 1059 and 1063 encouraged priests to live together in small communities in a way which conformed to monastic ideals, but without withdrawing from the world behind the walls of an enclosure in the way that monks did. By 1150, almost all of these groups had adopted a rule of life written by Augustine, the great Western theologian of the fifth century. Such priests became known as Augustinian Canons, abbreviated to Austin Canons, or Black Canons after their habit of wearing a hooded black cloak over a black cassock.

The Augustinian order first established itself in England at Colchester, around 1106, and spread rapidly. In time, there were over two hundred houses in England and Wales, more than any other order in medieval England. The canons gave up private property and lived a communal life, although under a less severe discipline than the monks. They frequently conducted a pastoral ministry. Some of their communities in London took on the care of the sick, and both Saint Thomas's and Saint Bartholomew's Hospitals in London were Augustinian foundations.

Repton Priory

The first Augustinian community in our area was set up at Repton. Although the abbey had been destroyed in the ninth century, the church had somehow survived the invasion of the pagan Danes with its shrine of St. Wystan intact. H.M. Taylor points to the wearing of the stone steps in the stairways leading from the church down into the crypt, which had been cut through the masonry to accommodate large numbers of visitors on special occasions, as witness to its popularity during the tenth century . Ironically, it was a later Christian Danish King, Cnut (1016-35), who brought this to an end. An enthusiastic collector of relics, he had the remains moved to a new shrine at Evesham.

The church of Repton was granted to the Augustinian Canons of Calke, in Derbyshire, around 1053, by Maud widow of Ranulph, fourth earl of Chester, lady of the manor of Repton, on condition that the canons transfer their chief

The seal of the Priory of Repton.

residence to Repton. The main body of the canons moved there in 1172, when Maud had erected priory buildings. She stipulated that Calke should continue as a cell of Repton. The canons of Holy Trinity inherited the lands of Calke at Repton, Kegworth, Ticknall, Tamworth and other places, and came to control other lands in Derbyshire, Nottinghamshire and Leicestershire, and several churches in Essex.

The priory drew all the income of the parish church and, rather than appointing a vicar, the canons staffed the church and its chapels themselves. It is clear that they wished to use the church to exploit the fame of their predecessors. They acquired a small portion of the remains of Saint Wystan from Evesham, and claimed to possess the bell of Saint Guthlac, another Saxon saint associated with the old abbey. Guthlac had been received there by the Abbess Alfritha about 696. A few years later, he travelled down the Trent by boat to Croyland, where he became a hermit. His bell was placed on the heads of pilgrims as a cure for headaches.

Like many monasteries, Repton came to be burdened with providing pensions for the servants of the mighty. For example, in 1263 Pope Urban IV 'granted permission' to Master John de Ebulo, papal sub-deacon and chaplain, to hold a pension of forty silver marks from the priory. This was a blatant example of pluralism, for this well-connected priest already enjoyed the incomes of three English and two continental churches. By contrast, in 1327, Robert of Driffeld, who had served the king and his father over many years in the royal kitchens, was sent to Repton Priory as a pensioner.

Linda Owen

Remains of Repton Priory, looking towards the school.

During the reign of Edward III Robert Tebbe, one of the canons, was accused 'of many crimes which it would be too shameful to relate'. The prior claimed that a penance much lighter than he really deserved, had been imposed on him, but that despite this he had left the house. He was going around in secular clothes with his friends, armed with bow and arrows, and threatening to harm the canons and set fire to their barns. J. C. Cox thought that he might have been behind a violent attack on the priory during a visitation by Bishop Stretton in November, 1364. While the bishop was in the chapter-house 'certain satellites of Satan - the whole community of the town - bearing swords and staves, and bows and arrows, came with much noise and tumult, and villainously hindered and alarmed the bishop and his clerks'. They attacked one of the episcopal retinue at the gates and then broke them down. Then they besieged the priory buildings until the next day, shooting through the windows 'so that they could none of them go out without fear of death or at least of grievous bodily harm'. Members of the local gentry arrived and restored order.

The bishop then pronounced the sentence of greater excommunication on everyone in Repton, and placed the entire town under an interdict. The former was a process of expulsion from the Church accompanied by a solemn cursing 'by bell, book and candle', after which no Christian was supposed to communicate with them in any way. The latter was a ban upon the performance of any religious services for the people of the town. Those under an interdict might not be baptised, marry, nor bury their dead with Christian rites. Everyone was warned against having any communication with the people of Repton, and the sentence was announced in all the churches of diocese.

At the beginning of the sixteenth century religious observance at Repton was clearly lax, for in 1518 Bishop Geoffrey Blythe found that of thirteen canons available for the religious services, only three usually bothered to attend.

Left: Repton Priory, medieval gateway.

Below:
Remains of the medieval priory in the grounds of Repton School.

Linda Owen

Above: Repton Priory remains at Repton School.

Right and below: Medieval passageway and gateways.

Linda Owen

Linda Owen

Calwich Priory

This small community some five miles south-west of Ashbourne was originally founded between 1125 and 1130 as a cell of Kenilworth Priory, in Warwickshire, and dedicated to Saint Margaret. It was to contain four canons, one being appointed canon-in-charge by the prior of Kenilworth. Nicholas of Gresley and his wife Margery gave the income of the church of Longford for their support. By 1163 Longford Church had been exchanged for the more convenient church at Ellastone.

The right of the prior of Kenilworth to transfer canons whenever he liked soon led to dissatisfaction. Matters came to a head in 1334, during a dispute over pasture rights in Ellastone, when the canon-in-charge claimed to be prior of Calwich. He was immediately recalled by the prior of Kenilworth. But shortly afterwards, in 1349, Calwich was made an independent priory with the right to elect its own prior, and with the lord of the manor of Longford as patron. In return for its independence, the new priory was required to pay three pounds annually to Kenilworth Priory.

The small community must have found this payment onerous. In 1385 the prior petitioned to be excused paying tax on the grounds that the three canons then in residence were too old to work and too poor to hire others to work for them, except for their bare necessities. Since their petition was granted, it seems likely that there was some truth in their claim.

Fragments of dressed stone near the site of Calwich Priory.

Linda Owen

When the bishop inspected Calwich Priory in 1518, he found only two canons in residence: the prior and a single companion, John Dean. The latter had been professed at Trentham Priory, and J.C. Dickinson thought that he had probably been lured there in order to keep the community in existence. When the prior died, in 1531, there was only a single canon left.

Stone Priory

Stone Priory was probably founded between 1138 and 1147 by Robert II of Stafford, who at that time gave to the canons the manor of Horton, Saint Mary's castle chapel at Stafford with the services of a villein, the churches of Madeley, and half the church of Wootton Wawen, in Warwickshire with a mill, a villein with his holding and part of a wood in Wootton Wawen, and a share of the bounty of his hunting. This was also a daughter house of Kenilworth Priory, although Dickinson notes that it soon acquired semi-independent status because of its adoption by the barons of Stafford as their 'family monastery'.

Linda Owen

Vaulted chamber, probably the Chapter House of Stone Priory, in the cellars of "The Priory", Lichfield Street.

In 1263, during the period of upheaval caused by the Barons' War, a royalist force under William la Zouche and David, brother of Prince Llewellyn of Wales, occupied Stafford town and Chartley Castle. On their return from this expedition, they plundered Stone Priory and burned down the town. In August 1264, the tide of war turned, and Prior Roger of Worcester took advantage of the changed circumstances to recoup some of his losses. He attacked the lands of Hulton Abbey at Normacot and took three hundred head of sheep, impounding them at Stallington. When the abbot of Hulton went to court to obtain redress, the sheriff confessed himself unable to do anything on account of the disorder caused by the war.

In 1260 Kenilworth recognised the right of Stone as an independent house. During a vacancy custody of Stone Priory was to be exercised by one of the canons or servants of Kenilworth. The canons of Stone were to obtain a license from the prior of Kenilworth to elect a new prior, and two canons of Kenilworth were to be present at the election. The prior of Stone was free to receive and profess canons, and to dispose of its property at his discretion. The prior of Kenilworth was entitled to visit Stone and be received with hospitality with his train of ten horses for a two-day annual visit.

The property of Kenilworth and Stone was divided among them. Stone received the churches of Madeley, Milwich, the chapel of Saint Nicholas in Stafford Castle, half the church of Stoke-on-Trent, two churches in Warwickshire, and lands in Stone, Colwich, Sandon, Stafford and Warwickshire. In 1293 the prior also established his right, in virtue of a charter granted by King Henry I, to erect a gallows.

During the late thirteenth century the priory got into debt and defaulted on corrodies. Thus in 1294, William, son of Robert of Cotes, sued the prior for depriving him of a corrody consisting of a loaf of bread, a gallon of ale, broth, and the same ration of food as a canon received each day; two candles each night during November, December, and January; and each year four cartloads of wood, a robe worth one mark, and provisions for a horse and groom for three nights.

In 1312 the priory was granted a general licence to acquire lands and rents to the annual value of twenty pounds 'on account of the devotion which the king bears to St. Wulfad whose body rests in the church of the priory of Stone'. However, royal attentions were not always so benign. In 1315 the king burdened the priory with the maintenance for life of William of Blakelowe, a soldier who had been maimed at the siege of Carlisle.

The location of the priory on the main highway between Stafford and Chester led to many demands for hospitality upon the priory. For this reason, in 1343 the canons were allowed to appropriate the entire income of the church of Madeley. In 1446 the Pope agreed that the canons could themselves staff the church of Stone because priests were 'hard to find' and it was not distant from the house.

During the mid-fifteenth century, Prior Thomas Wyse (c.1439-73) got into a dispute over the income earned by the canons from their plots of land in the priory garden. He acted arrogantly, and their resentment grew, so that the community was divided by 'schisms...... insults, hard and unjust words...... prolonged malice and wickedness'. Three of the canons took their grievances to the archbishop's Court. A number of improvements in the administration of the priory were proposed, and the prior was asked to accept them. He refused, was excommunicated, and appealed to Rome.

In December 1450 a distinguished commission consisting of the abbots of Darley, in Derbyshire, Lilleshall, in Shropshire, Arbury, in Warwickshire and Ranton in Staffordshire, visited the priory. They found that any communal religious life had completely broken down, a development they attributed to the work of Satan himself. The prior was ordered to be modest and kind to the canons, and the members of the community to live in 'charity, peace and concord', and be obedient to the prior. Officials were to be appointed by the prior only on the advice of the community. Annual accounts were to be drawn up. The priory seal was to be kept in a box with three separate locks: one key each to be held by the prior, sub-prior and sacrist. Each canon was to receive a salary for clothing and other necessities. The profits of cultivation of the garden plots and from keeping bees were to be enjoyed in common, and no longer individually. The canons' shaving and laundry were to be paid for out of the common funds, and the canons were strictly forbidden to employ their own laundresses. It seems that the canons had been running their own businesses within the priory for personal profit.

The visitors also insisted on attendance at the monastic services. The priory officials must be personally present at least for matins, vespers and mass on each Sunday and important feast day. They ordered all the canons who were priests to say mass daily. Ordinary canons who missed matins, the midnight office, were to be punished by fines and a special punishment diet.

Meals were to be eaten in common in the prior's hall until the refectory had been repaired. Eating and drinking in the dormitory cells, which had been the practice, was forbidden, and only the infirm or those invited to the prior's table were to eat apart. There had been no proper provision for the old and infirm for some years. The visitors ordered an infirmary to he built, and an official to be appointed to take charge of it without delay. He was admonished to attend conscientiously to the needs of the sick, since 'a similar tiring may happen to him in the same way. And therefore let him do for another what he would wish to have done for himself'.

In the subsequent history of the priory, there is little indication of any real reformation. In 1458 a bishop had to bless the priory church after it had been polluted by bloodshed.

The episcopal visitations of 1518 and 1521 reveal a standing feud between the prior, Richard Dodicote, and the sub-prior. The prior had installed a glover named Onyon, together with his wife, son and daughters, in the bell tower, maintaining them at the expense of the community. The sub prior objected, and claimed that he had been threatened and attacked by Onyon and his son, and insulted by one of his daughters. He said that he thought that Onyon's wife was a thief, and that one of his daughters had 'suspect' access to the precincts. He also complained that the prior had persistently failed to repair a fence which allowed access to outsiders, and that he had caught one of the canons with the wife of a townsman. The rest of the community stood by the prior, charging the sub-prior with drunkenness and being too fond of hunting.

The community (including the prior) numbered nine or ten during the fourteenth century, but a visitation of 1518 records only six canons and two novices. This was considered by the visitor to be too low. The prior said that he wished to increase their numbers, but the others were unwilling to receive any more applicants, although by 1521 two more had been admitted.

Linda Owen

Linda Owen

Above:
Vaulted chamber, probably
the Chapter House of Stone
Priory, in the cellars of
"The Priory".

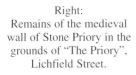

Right:
Remains of the medieval
wall of Stone Priory in the
grounds of "The Priory",
Lichfield Street.

Linda Owen

Rocester Abbey

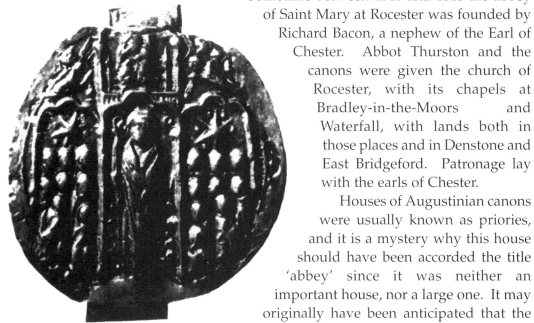

The seal of the Abbey of Rocester.

Sometime between 1141 and 1146 the abbey of Saint Mary at Rocester was founded by Richard Bacon, a nephew of the Earl of Chester. Abbot Thurston and the canons were given the church of Rocester, with its chapels at Bradley-in-the-Moors and Waterfall, with lands both in those places and in Denstone and East Bridgeford. Patronage lay with the earls of Chester.

Houses of Augustinian canons were usually known as priories, and it is a mystery why this house should have been accorded the title 'abbey' since it was neither an important house, nor a large one. It may originally have been anticipated that the Earl would later increase the endowments of the community, enabling it to be expanded, but this never happened.

In 1229, when Bishop Stavensby gave the abbey permission to appropriate the income of the church of Rocester, the canons were said to be suffering greater poverty than any others in the diocese. The grant was made on account of their 'immoderate poverty...... their holiness of life, their gravity of demeanour, and the grace of their virtuous religious life'. Of itself, this would have made their community unique in our area.

When the earldom of Chester was annexed to the Crown, the King became their patron. The nature of royal gifts indicates continued poverty. For example, in 1240, Henry III gave them money for clothing and for wine for the celebration of mass. In 1246 he provided them with a chalice. In 1284 Bishop Meuland discovered that the abbey was in debt, yet was providing poor travellers with hospitality beyond its means. The churches at Kingstone and Edensor, were added to the abbey's endowments to alleviate the situation. Unfortunately, the canons of Rocester were badly affected by the climate change at the beginning of the fourteenth century. In 1318 they claimed that cattle plague and bad harvests had reduced them to such poverty that they were obliged to go out begging.

This atmosphere of saintly poverty did not last. In 1334 the abbot complained that one of his canons, sent to the king's court on business, was wandering around the countryside in possession of important abbey documents and spending the community's money. In 1337 the abbot and canon Geoffrey Spagurnel were both accused, together with a number of laymen, of breaking into Bolingbroke Castle, temporarily imprisoning countess Alice of Lincoln, and taking away twenty horses. In 1375, another canon, Richard of Foston, was accused of travelling the country posing as the abbot, while the abbot himself, John Cheswardine, was accused of harbouring the murderers of William Verneye. By 1385 the abbot had established his innocence, and there was a warrant out for the arrest of Richard of Foston and two other canons of Rocester, Walter Osbern and Robert of Bakewell. It is likely that the canons had expelled their abbot and were determined to replace him. Evidently they were successful, for in 1386 Abbot Cheswardine resigned and Robert of Bakewell was elected in his place.

In 1524 the house was being efficiently run, although it was sixty pounds in debt. Instead of the usual half dozen or so canons, there were nine in residence at that time. Observance of the rule of life was described as satisfactory, although there was said to be some dissension within the community, and the canons spent a lot of time in alehouses.

Lilleshall Abbey

The seal of the Abbey of Lilleshall

Although it was an Augustinian house, the origins of Lilleshall Abbey are rather different from that of the other houses of the order. Under abbot Gervaise (1121-47), the Augustinian canons of Saint-Nicholas in Arrouaise adopted many of the strict practices of the new Cistercian Order, so that Arrouaise and its daughter houses, such as Dorchester Abbey, in Oxfordshire, came to be regarded for some time as a separate order.

Philip and Richard of Belmeis awarded land around 1143 at Lizard, some two miles south east of the present site, to found a daughter house of Dorchester Abbey. The soil was poor, and the community relocated to Donnington Wood. After Richard of Belmeis had secured for his canons the income of a college of priests attached to Saint Alkmund's Church, Shrewsbury, they moved to Lilleshall.

Although effectively independent, the community of St. Mary's Abbey, Lilleshall retained some of the distinctive features of its Arrouaisian origins. Since St. Alkmund's had been a royal foundation, the abbey which inherited its lands was regarded as under royal patronage.

This became a well-endowed and prosperous house, as may be seen from the number of granges established. In addition to a home grange, outlying farms were set up at Cheswell, Watling Street, Wealdmoor, Atcham, Albrightlee, Blackfordby, Burlington, Charlton, Grindlow, Lizard, Longdon-upon-Tern, Preston Gubballs, and Uckington.

A tannery was set up on the abbey site, where cattle and horse hides would have been treated with oak bark to produce leather. The process was finished with the application of oil and tallow to make the leather supple and waterproof. Despite the unpleasant smell which was inevitably a by-product of this process, a site close to the conventual buildings seems to have been customary.

A fishery was set up at Atcham, and salt pans in Nantwich were leased for rent. The abbey was authorised to collect tolls at Atcham on the road to Holyhead. From 1471 the abbey held the patronage of a leper hospital dedicated to St. John in Bridgenorth.

Henry III visited the house in 1241 and 1245 on hunting trips. On his way to a parliament held in Shrewsbury, Richard II stayed there over 24th-26th January, 1398. He reportedly arrived not only with the Queen, but also accompanied by five dukes, four earls, and three bishops with their retinues. For some time a fraternity of rich laymen existed whose members would, for a payment of course, be included in the regular prayers of the canons. After a bout of illness, in January 1398 John of Gaunt spent several days at the abbey and was enrolled as a member.

Despite its comparative wealth, the climate changes at the beginning of the fourteenth century, the scattered nature of its estates, which made them difficult to administer, together with the usual managerial incompetence, brought a short period of financial hardship. A visitation by Bishop Roger Northburgh (1322-58) complained that no accounts had been kept, and the abbey was in debt. The abbot sold corrodies, freed serfs and sold wood on his own authority, without consulting the community. The lay steward was wasting the property of the house and some of the officials were useless and should be dismissed.

When Abbot John of Chetwynd resigned, he quarrelled with his successor, and with his supporters attacked the abbey and carried off some of its goods. The king installed administrators to fend off ruin. A later visitation reported no improvement. The abbot at that time, Henry of Stoke, was too old and infirm to function properly. In particular, he was wasting valuable wood by allowing trees fit for use as timber to be cut down for their branches or burned for charcoal.

In 1521 there were nine canons and two novices in residence, and the abbey was in debt once more. In the opinion of visitors, too many lay persons lived in the house; a schoolmaster was employed in a small school within the monastery for the sons of gentlemen, and several of the canons were associating with women of ill-repute. The canons themselves complained about the food.

Remains of the Abbey Church, Lilleshall.

Linda Owen

Linda Owen

Linda Owen

Linda Owen

Above: Slype, Lilleshall Abbey.

Linda Owen

Right and below: Grave slabs.

Linda Owen

Linda Owen

Lilleshall Abbey, the Priory Church.
Norman archways.

Linda Owen

Trentham Priory

Linda Owen

The chancel of Trentham Parish Church
incorporating part of the priory church.

The priory of St. Mary and All Saints, Trentham, was founded by Ranulf de Gernon, Earl of Chester, some time before his death in 1153. The new community was granted the manor of Trentham together with Blurton and Cocknage, and the church of Trentham, with its chapels at Newcastle-under-Lyme and Barlaston. On the death of Earl Ranulf, patronage passed to the king. Further acquisitions included property in Newcastle-under-Lyme, Clayton Griffin, Longton, Barlaston, Betley, Balterley, Wall Grange, in Leek, and Elkstone, and the churches of Trusley and Sutton-on-the-Hill in Derbyshire.

During the late thirteenth and early fourteenth centuries, the earls of Lancaster claimed patronage of the priory as part of their manor of Newcastle-under-Lyme, a claim which was resisted by the Crown. This dispute caused endless problems for the canons. Whenever a prior died, the agents of the earls of Lancaster were likely to occupy the priory, collect its rents, cut down its trees and help themselves to its goods. In 1344, after their particularly aggressive acts following the death of prior Richard of Dilhorne, the house was placed under royal protection, Ralph, Lord Stafford, being entrusted with its safety.

In return for this protection the canons, who usually numbered seven or eight, were regularly required to provide free food and lodging to retired royal servants and soldiers.

An embarrassing incident took place during the visitation of Bishop Geoffrey Blythe, in 1525, when the prior accused himself of having carnal relations with women. The other canons explained that he was senile, and unable to function effectively as head of the community.

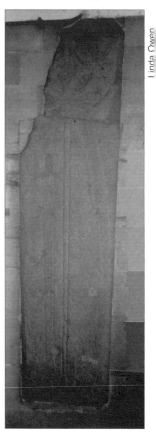

Linda Owen

Medieval grave slab built into a wall
of Trentham Parish Church.

Ranton Priory

The priory of Ranton, some six miles west of Stafford, was founded during the mid twelfth century by Robert fitz Noel of Ellenhall. The foundation charter indicates that the site was built on land cleared from the forest. In addition, Robert gave land, the church and a mill in Coton Clanford in Seighford, and the church of Grandborough, in Warwickshire. The canons were a colony from Haughmond Abbey, in Shropshire.

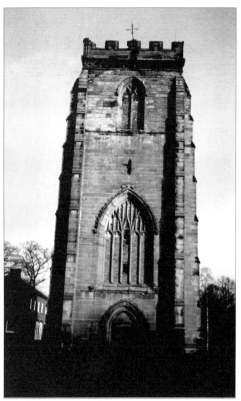

Linda Owen

Ranton Priory, the Tower.

Robert's son, Thomas, added land in Seighford, Ranton, and Coton Clanford, and arranged to be buried in the priory church. Richard of Harcourt of Great Sheepy, in Leicestershire, gave land in Great Sheepy, fishing rights and rent from his mill in what was to become the priory's most important estate outside Staffordshire. Later gifts included land in Longford, in Shropshire, wasteland in Eccleshall, and several small grants from successive heads of the Knightley family in the late twelfth and early thirteenth centuries.

By the thirteenth century a hospital dedicated to St. Anne had been established within the priory precincts.

During the latter half of that century there were several disputes with the Doyly family, lords of Ranton. Some, over lands and rights of pasture in Ranton, J. C. Dickinson thought were due to conflicts arising from the clearing of waste. Others were over watercourses supplying the priory's mills and fishponds, and a private chapel the Doyly family had set up.

This priory developed commercial interests in the later thirteenth century in Stafford, Newcastle-under-Lyme, and Newport, in Shropshire, where they had property. Newport lay on the road from Stafford to Wales, and was probably used by personnel travelling to and from Wales on business, for at about this time Griffith ap Gwenwynwyn, Lord of Southern Powys, gave the priory the right to trade without paying tolls in his markets.

The canons of Ranton enjoyed the status of canons in the mother house at Haughmond, and were able to participate in the election of abbots there. The abbot of Haughmond had the duty to visit Ranton each year, but the canons were able to admit new members to their community on their own authority, although all had to profess obedience to the abbot. When there was a vacancy in the leadership of the community at Ranton, the canons would put forward two names, one of their

Ranton Priory

Right: Doorway.

Below:
The Tower. Traces of demolished Priory buildings
can be seen on the left photograph.

brethren and a canon of Haughmond, and the abbot would make the final choice.

During the mid-fourteenth century the bishop was attacked while conducting a visitation of Ranton Priory by John, son of Robert of Knightley, and others. He reported that they tried to prevent him from exercising his jurisdiction, besieging him with his retinue inside the priory, so that none of them dared to leave to buy food or other necessities. Afterwards their attackers hid in a wood, and when the bishop and his retinue emerged, they were ambushed as they tried to get back to the safety of the bishop's manor of Haywood. The bishop claimed that without the aid of people from the neighbourhood he would have been killed. As it was he had been robbed, and one of his servants assaulted.

The community usually numbered six canons. From the latter half of the fourteenth century the church of Seighford was staffed

Ranton Priory, architectural detail.

by one of their number, although in 1530 Bishop Blythe refused to institute the candidate nominated at that time by the prior because he was 'unlearned and unworthy'.

The prior himself complained in 1515 of the low standard of behaviour of three of his canons. Two of them, Robert Parker and Humphrey Huett, had each fathered a child. They were also in the habit of leaving the priory to go hunting without permission. The visitor ordered the prior to report their names to the bishop so that they could be transferred somewhere else. Nothing had been done six years later, and Huett was still leading an 'irregular life'.

St Thomas Priory, Stafford

Gerard fitz Brian, a burgess of Stafford, founded the priory of Saint Thomas the Martyr some time before 1175 on some land two miles south-east of Stafford on the banks of the Sow, which he leased from bishop Richard Peche of Lichfield. The first canons were drawn from Darley Abbey, in Derbyshire. The priory was initially endowed with some properties in the town of Stafford.

To this the bishop added properties in Lichfield, rights of pasture in Baswich, Orberton and Eccleshall, fishing rights on the Sow and Penk, and the right to gather wood on Cannock Chase. Bishop Peche came to regard himself as the founder of the priory, and when he retired in 1192, he entered St. Thomas as an ordinary canon, dying there later that year.

Little by little, this priory came to acquire a surprising amount of land and properties from various donors. Many were small, but the income they produced mounted up, and several donations of land in Whitgreave and Maer enabled the priory to build up significant estates there. Moreover, these grants continued long after the fashion for making such gifts to religious houses had passed.

For example, in 1277-8, John of Pendeford sold his manor of Pendeford in Tettenhall to the priory. He had committed an offence against the forest laws, fled abroad, and then returned to take refuge in the priory. A condition of the sale was that he could lodge within the precincts, and would receive a pension of 40s a year until his death.

As a result of the many bequests it received, in time, this priory became wealthier than the average house of its order, an achievement unique for any religious house in Staffordshire. A condition of some of the donations was that the donor and his heirs should have the right to present a canon to reside in the priory, and it seems likely that younger sons of the benefactors would have

The seal of the Priory of St Thomas, Stafford.

been prime candidates. The explanation for the number of donations and the subsequent wealth of this house seems to be that it came to be recognised a suitable home for landless sons of the wealthier gentry.

As was customary, the canons were sometimes required to provide for the old age of retired royal servants and others. But when, in 1280, Bishop Meuland demanded that the priory pay his barber a pension of two pounds a year, Archbishop Pecham condemned the demand as sacrilegious, and forbade the prior to comply.

In 1518, it was recorded that the prior ruled the community autocratically and unfairly but efficiently, although he relied too much on the advice of one of the canons, Richard Hervy, and certain laymen. The inventory of the priory's wealth was not read out before the entire community as it should have been, but only before an inner group of favourites. Some of the canons would eat with the prior rather than in the common refectory and did not sleep in the dormitory, but enjoyed their own private accommodation. The prior's servants did not show proper respect to the ordinary canons. There were too many hunting dogs. The bishop ordered the prior to put these things right and to increase the number of canons. Another visitation in 1524 showed that nothing had been done.

St Thomas' Priory,
Stafford

Left:
Medieval cellars in
Priory Farm showing
tiled floor.

Below right: Medieval stonework incorporated
into Priory Farm.
Below: Ancient doorway leading to the cellars.

Linda Owen

Outbuildings and walls of Priory Farm showing the incorporated stonework of St Thomas' Priory, Stafford.

Brewood (White Ladies) Priory

This community of nuns dedicated to Saint Leonard and following the rule of Saint Augustine was set up at some time during the late twelfth century across the Shropshire border, near Brewood. Like many nuns of this order, the sisters dressed in white habits, and so are sometimes confused with the Cistercians.

The community, which usually numbered about half a dozen, held modest holdings made up of scattered parcels of land in the neighbourhood, and further afield in Shropshire and Nottinghamshire. The canonesses lived on the rents they drew for these.

Members of the La Zouche family were benefactors of the community, and one Elizabeth la Zouche was prioress in 1314, illustrating once more the use to which the rich put the nunneries in providing for their unmarried daughters. Unusually, each of the nuns at the White Ladies Convent received an individual salary.

In 1338 the prioress was reprimanded for extravagance. Money had been spent on luxuries, and she kept hounds for hunting. In 1521 two of the nuns complained that their salaries were in arrears. In 1525 it was alleged that two of the cannonesses were regularly receiving letters from a monk of Dieulacres, and refusing to show them to the prioress as the rule demanded.

Linda Owen

A detail of the ruins of White Ladies' Priory, near Brewood.

Linda Owen

White Ladies' Priory, near Brewood.

White Ladies' Priory, near Brewood.

Linda Owen

Linda Owen

The 'Definitory' in the Cistercian Abbey of Citeaux, France.
In this room the preparations for the annual meetings of the Chapters-General were made, and the execution of the decisions of the assembled abbots coordinated.

chapter four
the reformed orders

At the end of the eleventh century there was a religious revival in France among monks who believed that the existing monasteries had become too wealthy, and too lax, to provide the environment for a truly religious life.

The White Monks

In 1098, Abbot Robert of Molesme, left his monastery to found a new community at Citeaux, near Dijon, in Eastern France. He and his successors, known as Cistercians, lived by a very strict interpretation of the Benedictine Rule. Warm underclothing and furs were forbidden. Meat, fish, eggs, cheese, white bread and butter were not to be served in the refectory. In order to isolate themselves from the surrounding world, the Cistercians resolved not to accept any income from churches or gifts of settled lands, which might incur obligations or responsibilities outside the monasteries.

This Spartan way of life attracted many adherents, and new monasteries following the stricter interpretation of the Rule were set up in remote places. Their churches were appropriately austere, with gold ornaments, stained glass windows and silk vestments specifically forbidden. The time spent at worship was shortened in favour of manual labour; although rather inconsistently, in addition to the choir monks, a class of lay brothers was introduced to perform most of the manual labour. These second-class members of the community took vows like the monks, but lived in their own inferior accommodation, and were strictly forbidden to learn how to read, lest they should become discontented with the station in life to which God had called them.

Under the third abbot of Citeaux, the Englishman Stephen Harding, a distinctive organisation was developed. Because they were exempt from inspection by the bishops, and in order to avoid the problems caused to traditional monasteries by incompetent or criminal abbots, 'daughter houses' were to be subjected to annual visitations by the 'father abbot' of the founding monastery. In addition, a Chapter-General, or assembly of all the abbots, was to be held each year at Citeaux, where an erring abbot or community could be subjected to discipline by the heads of the other houses of the order.

Saint Bernard of Clairvaux. Portrait in the treasury of the Cathedral, Troyes.

The Cistercians might have remained an obscure movement but for St. Bernard, who arrived along with about thirty of his relatives and friends in 1112 or 1113. In 1115 he founded a new abbey at Clairvaux. His charismatic leadership, fame and writings ensured the spectacular growth of the order. In 1128 the first Cistercian house was founded in England at Waverley, in Surrey, and most of the Cistercian monasteries in England were set up within the next thirty years, including Fountains, Rievaulx, and Tintern, located in remote valleys.

With compact estates, and with a large, disciplined labour force of lay brothers, the Cistercians were able to develop agriculture without having to take account of the traditional rights and customs of the serfs. In reclaiming marginal land

A page from an antiphonal, one of the service books used in a medieval monastery containing the music for the chant.

and in increasing production, especially that of wool in the large pastures of Wales and Yorkshire, the Cistercians played a large role in bringing about considerable progress during the twelfth century in the development of new techniques of farming, industry and commerce.

Radmore Abbey

At some time during the late 1130s, King Stephen granted Radmore to a small group of men who wished to become hermits in Cannock forest. Bishop Roger de Clinton gave them permission to follow any monastic rule they wished. A civil war was raging at the time, and to safeguard their position the hermits sought a charter from King Stephen's rival, the empress Maud. The first Cistercians had recently arrived in the country, and she persuaded them to adopt their rule.

The new monks received several grants of land, mostly in Warwickshire. William Croc, the steward of Cannock Forest, gave them all his rights in Great Wryley, in Cannock, on condition that he himself be admitted into the order. In 1153, Duke Henry of Normandy, Maud's son, gave them lands near Cannock. At the same time, he granted most of the royal lands in Staffordshire to the Earl of Chester, who promptly handed over Cannock town to the monks to finance the erection of monastic buildings.

A distinctive feature of monastic organisation pioneered by the Cistercians was the establishment of granges: outlying farmsteads where lay brothers cultivated arable land. The monks of Radmore set up a grange at Radway, in Warwickshire. The custom soon arose that the men of Radmore travelling to and from Radway Grange would break their journey to enjoy the hospitality of the Cistercians of a new abbey at Bordesley, in Worcestershire, and a very strong relationship soon developed between the two communities.

The monks of Radmore quickly grew unhappy with their situation in Cannock Forest, where they were frequently intimidated by royal foresters. They secured from King Henry II, at his coronation in December 1154, the royal manor of Stoneleigh, in Worcestershire, in return for surrendering Radmore to him, and in June 1155 the community left Staffordshire for their new home.

The Grey Monks

The Cistercians were not the only reforming order founded at the end of the eleventh century. In 1093, Vitalis of Tierceville, a priest in the retinue of Robert Curthose, Duke of Normandy, the son of William the Conqueror, became the focus of a religious movement in the forest of Mortain, on the borders of Normandy, Maine and Brittany in Western France. By 1115 Raoul II, the Lord of Fougères had endowed it as the abbey of Savigny.

Vitalis's successor, Abbot Geoffrey, began a period of ambitious expansion and organisation on the same pattern as that of the Cistercians. The 'grey monks' of Savigny rapidly expanded throughout northern France. Their first community in England settled at Tulketh, in Lancashire, in 1124, moving to Furness three years later. During the next twenty years, ten more Savigniac monasteries were set up in England.

This dramatic expansion very quickly brought severe problems. Effective control of the daughter houses could no longer be maintained by their mother houses, and by the 1140s the Savigniac houses of England were notorious for indiscipline and low morale. Most of the abbots no longer bothered to attend annual Chapters-General, and many of the monks openly demanded to return to France.

Due to the influence of St. Bernard, the prestige of the Cistercians was at its height at this time. Abbot Serlo of Savigny himself intended to retire to Clairvaux in his old age. A merger was decided upon whereby all the Savigniac monasteries would be incorporated within the Cistercian order. In 1157, Abbot Serlo surrendered all his monasteries to the abbot of Citeaux; the Savigniac monks exchanged their grey habits for the white robes of the Cistercians and adopted the rule of the Cistercian order. Only the monks of Furness objected, but they were compelled to submit by Pope Eugenius III, himself a Cistercian monk.

As might have been expected, this union failed to inspire the communities of Savigniac foundation with the zeal of the Cistercians, and long after the union those Cistercian houses which were daughter foundations of Savigny could still be distinguished from the other Cistercian monasteries by their slackness. All the Cistercian foundations in or near Staffordshire, saving only Radmore, were of Savigniac origin.

Combermere Abbey

In 1133, some fourteen years before the union of the two orders, Hugh of Malbanc (Nantwich), a follower of Earl Ranulph II de Gernon of Chester, provided the necessary endowment of land for the foundation of the third Savigniac house to be founded in England, at Combermere, in Cheshire, near the Shropshire border. The foundation charter was witnessed by Earl Ranulf, and Hugh wished the Earl to be the principal guardian of the abbey.

Hugh endowed the monks with lands in the south of the county on the borders of Shropshire and Staffordshire: the manor of Wilkesley and other lands, and the churches of Alstonfield and Sandon in Staffordshire. The monastery later acquired the manor of Drayton, the church of Acton, with its chapels in Nantwich, Wrenbury and Church Minshull, and various lands, properties, tithes and rents. Granges were set up at Wincle, Cliff, Shifford, Chesthill, Yarlett, Cotes and Newton.

Despite an initial period of prosperity when several daughter houses were

Clearing the forest.
From a 12th century manuscript at Citeaux.

Monks working as carpenters, from a 12th century manuscript in the Vatican Library.

founded, the story of this monastery is one of disaster following upon disaster. By 1275 the community had fallen into debt, and the bishop of Bath and Wells was given custody of the abbey. In 1276 it was taken under royal administration for a time.

In 1281 the abbot was in dispute with the archbishop of Canterbury over the church of Drayton. When the archbishop tried to inspect the church, the abbot and six monks barred his entry. The archbishop complained that the monks had 'defended it like a castle', placed them under a ban of excommunication, and put Combermere Abbey under an interdict. News of these events reached the Chapter-General in France. It is not known when these measures were lifted, but in 1283 the monks were excused from contributing supplies to a royal expedition against the Welsh on the grounds that they had insufficient food for their own use. Combermere was once more placed under royal administration.

Early in the fourteenth century the abbey came under pressure from hostile neighbours. In March 1309 Richard of Fullshurst and a band of armed men assaulted the abbot in Nantwich, killed the prior, the abbot's deputy, burned down the abbey's property there, and stole goods worth two hundred pounds. While the case was still pending, Fullshurst again attacked the abbot and his servants, this time in his house, killing three horses and stealing sixty pounds. There may have been a version of this story to which we do not have access in the surviving records, for Fullshurst demanded that the abbot of Savigny set up an enquiry into the affairs of Abbot Robot, which he did. Because he lived in constant fear of ambush by his enemies, Abbot Robot appealed to King Edward II, and the King ordered everybody to leave him

Linda Owen

Combermere Hall, incorporating part of the fabric of the abbey buildings.

alone. Whatever its cause, this dispute led to a long standing vendetta, for in 1360 the then abbot of Combermere was accused of attacking the property of Sir Robert Fullshurst.

The finances of Combermere did not improve. In 1314 the abbot leased Cotes Grange to Burton Abbey for twenty-eight years in return for their paying off a huge debt of eight hundred pounds. Yet, on account of its 'poverty and miserable state', the Crown took the abbey into custody again in 1315. The keepers were ordered, after setting aside reasonable allowances for the abbot and his monks, to use the remaining income to meet debts and to repair the fabric of the buildings.

In 1328 the abbot pleaded that Combermere was unable to maintain the customary hospitality which monasteries were expected to provide to visitors, due to the mismanagement of his predecessor. During the previous twenty years many of the lands of the monastery had been leased out on terms extremely disadvantageous to the abbey.

An indication of the extent to which the monasteries suffered from the Black Death was given when the Black Prince ordered the justiciar of Chester to protect the remaining monks of the Cheshire abbeys from being burdened by frequent visits of local folk requiring hospitality. Yet in the very next year, the same Black Prince demanded that one of his servants be appointed abbey porter, and later insisted that Combermere accept two corrodians or pensioners.

By 1410 the abbey was so much in debt that the monks pleaded that they would not be able to feed themselves if they were forced to pay everything they owed. The debts were blamed on past maladministration, which had allowed the buildings to get into such a state of bad repair that it would cost one thousand pounds to restore them. In 1412 the abbey was administered by officials of the County Palatine. This constant indebtedness clearly required an imaginative solution, and there is evidence that Abbot William Plymouth was not lacking in initiative, for in 1414 he was accused of counterfeiting gold coins.

In 1417, Richard Hoggeson of Holyhurst and Richard Tenche of Lodmore were accused of holding the abbey by force against the orders of the king and the will of the abbot, attacking royal officers, and carrying off into Shropshire some of the abbey treasures. These included books valued at one hundred pounds, together with the abbey seal. They used the seal to forge documents in their favour. They may have simply been trying to recover debts owed to them, for the two were subsequently acquitted. Later, Hoggeson and one of the monks were outlawed, and the abbot deposed. Anne J. Kettle thought that this is all explained by some feud within the monastery itself, which seems quite likely.

In 1435 one of the abbey tenants in Nantwich, John Kingesley, was accused of extorting money from the abbot over a period of many years. In 1446 Abbot Richard Alderwas was killed by a labourer at Dodcott.

In 1520 one of the abbot's servants murdered one of the monks. According to the dead man's brother, the abbot tried to hush the matter up on the grounds that 'this abbey is already in an evil name for using of misrule'. Everyone was sworn to secrecy and the corpse was hidden for six months inside the abbey. When this was reported to Thomas Cromwell, he ominously warned that if a suitably 'discreet' person were not put in charge of Combermere, serious consequences would follow.

Linda Owen

The Lodge, Combermere Hall.

Linda Owen

The choir stalls of Nantwich Church, said by tradition to be from Combermere Abbey.

Opposite page: Detail of the choir stalls.

Linda Owen

Linda Owen

Linda Owen

Linda Owen

Croxden Abbey

In 1176 Bertram of Verdun, Lord of Alton, granted lands for the foundation of a daughter house of the abbey of Aunay-sur-Odon, in Normandy, itself a Savigniac foundation. An Englishman was chosen to be the first abbot, and the community moved to Cotton. Three years later they moved a few miles further south, to Croxden, in the fertile valley of the Churnet. The site at Cotton may have proved inhospitable, although F. A. Hibbert argued that the settlement at Cotton was probably never intended to be more than a temporary arrangement. The buildings erected at Croxden show evidence of the French origin of the monks in the fashionable semi-circular apse built at the east end of the church.

The monks were given Bertram's lands at Croxden, Alton, Checkley, Uttoxeter, Musden, and Codsall in Staffordshire. They also received grants of land in Leicestershire and Derbyshire, a salt pan at Middlewich, in Cheshire, and a mill at Stamford, in Lincolnshire. Further lands were added later, including lands in Cheadle from Rose of Verdun, and rights over churches at Alton and at Tugby, in Leicestershire.

The monks' treatment of one gift shows the way in which they were prepared to trade bequests so as to make the most of their endowments. In 1199 King John gave them lands in Ireland. These were obviously inconveniently distant, and he was persuaded to swap them in 1200 for an annuity of £5. In 1205 this was in turn exchanged for land in Edgemond in Shropshire. Still dissatisfied, the men of Croxden swapped this for Caldon Grange in 1287, with the Shropshire Cistercian abbey of Buildwas.

Granges were set up at Musden, Oaken, Riston, Caldon and Cheadle. The thirteenth and fourteenth centuries were periods of great prosperity. Croxden Abbey was soon selling more wool to Flemish and Italian merchants than any other house in our area. This Abbey was responsible for considerable destruction of the remaining woodlands for timber and charcoal. Between 1291 and 1336 alone, the *Croxden Chronicle* records the burning down of eight woods for charcoal, which was then sold.

Fish were farmed extensively in various locations, although an account of what was found when one of the ponds was drained in 1300 suggests that eels were the main stock, and this is supported by evidence from monasteries elsewhere in the kingdom. Since they were not fish, they were not covered by the strict rules of fasting.

The evidence of gross mismanagement and consequent penury so evident at Combermere is absent at Croxden. Discipline seems to have been unusually good. When Thomas Hody, who was lodging in the abbey, was killed in a fight between grooms in the stable one night in 1274, the abbot promptly dismissed his entire household of servants.

Theoretically, each Cistercian abbot had to travel to Citeaux every year to attend the annual meeting of the Chapter-General. The history of Croxden shows how onerous this journey must have been, particularly for elderly or ailing men. Abbot

William of Ashbourne died on September 22nd 1237 on his way back from the meeting, and was buried abroad. Abbot William of Houton died at Dijon in 1274, and was buried at Citeaux. Abbot William of Over was deposed by the Chapter-General in 1308 for failing to obey the summons to attend.

Relations between the monks and their patrons, the Verduns, were usually very good, but when, through the failure of the male line, the lordship of Alton passed to Thomas de Furnivalle, problems quickly arose. Thomas insisted that the monks distribute alms at the abbey gate every day. In addition, he demanded that seven of his bailiffs be fed every Friday in a room especially set aside for the purpose, and that the monastery be used to stable his horses and hunting dogs. When the monks objected he became petty, taking one of their farm carts and only releasing it after the abbot went to court to obtain a writ. He hid a hundred and sixty sheep from Musden Grange in his park for seven weeks. He seized twenty oxen and thirty horses and took them to Wootton Park, so that the ploughing and sowing could not be done. Things got so bad that the monks barricaded themselves inside the abbey by erecting two fences inside the main gates, and used a small door in the far wall of the enclosure to enter and leave. Eventually they followed the advice of the local gentry, and took Furnivall to court. This must have settled the matter, for in 1321 the abbot baptised his daughter.

Despite its generally sound administration, Croxden did not entirely escape financial problems. The climate changes at the beginning of the fourteenth century, together with a degree of mismanagement, prompted the mother house of Auney to send a commission which deposed Abbot Alexander of Colbeley in 1368. In 1405 royal permission was given for the monks to appoint members of their own community as vicars of Alton. This was an unusual procedure for Cistercians and strictly against the rules of their order, but the impoverishment of the abbey was cited in justification. Following the Black Death there was usually an abbot and six monks at Croxden, but by the beginning of the sixteenth century there were twelve again, probably the original number.

Linda Owen

The Cellarer's Range and the Nave, Croxden Abbey.

Linda Owen

Croxden Abbey

Top left:
The Abbey Church from the north.

Bottom: The Slype.

Bottom right:
There is evidence of repeated rebuilding.

Linda Owen

Linda Owen

Entrances to the Library, Chapter House and Monks' Parlour.

Linda Owen

The Abbey Church.

Linda Owen

The Nave from the Cloister Hearth.

Linda Owen

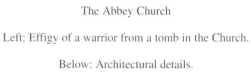

Linda Owen

Linda Owen

Linda Owen

Linda Owen

Linda Owen

The Abbey Church

Left: Effigy of a warrior from a tomb in the Church.

Below: Architectural details.

Dieulacres Abbey

The seal of the Abbey of Dieulacres

According to the Dieulacres Chronicle, the origins of this abbey, in Leek, lie in a vision of his dead grandfather that Earl Ranulph III de Blundeville of Chester thought he had received in a dream. The apparition informed the Earl that Pope Innocent III would place England under an interdict, and that in the seventh year of the ban he was to found a Cistercian monastery at Cholpesdale, in Leek, on the site of a chapel of the Virgin Mary. He was to do this by transferring to Leek the Cistercian monks of the Abbey of Poulton, in Cheshire.

Poulton Abbey, a daughter house of Combermere, had been founded by Robert Pincerna, hereditary butler of Earl Ranulph II, when his master, who had supported the Empress Matilda in the Civil War, had been imprisoned by King Stephen. Earls Ranulph II and Hugh II gave them lands in Cheshire, in Middlewich, Poulton, Alderley, Davenham, Aldford, Great Budworth, Over, and Prestbury; and in Staffordshire at Swythamley, and fishing rights on the Dee. This community was in constant danger of raids by the Welsh, and Ranulph III decided to appease his grandfather's ghost by transferring the community to Leek in accordance with his wishes.

Michael Fisher suggests that the chapel at Leek referred to in the dream may have been a hermitage situated in a small grotto close to the site of the abbey, which shows signs of having once been divided into separate sections and provided with a door. The Chronicle records two traditions, not necessarily incompatible, concerning the origin of the name 'Dieulacres'. When the Earl told his wife about his dream she exclaimed in Norman French 'Deux encres' at which the Earl said that it should be called Dieulencres. Alternatively, as he laid the foundation stone he murmured 'Deux l'encres', meaning in English, 'May God increase it'. In time it became known as the monastery of Dieulacres.

To lands already held by Poulton Abbey, Ranulph added the manor and church of Leek and its chapels, mills at Leek and Hume, a salt pan at Middlewich, and pasture at Rossall, on the Lancashire coast. Poulton Abbey was reduced to the status of a grange of the monastery of Dieulacres. New granges were established in Staffordshire at Westwood, Foker, Birchall, Meerbrook and Swythamley.

When the monks arrived, Leek was already a significant market town with the right to hold a market every Wednesday and an annual eight-day fair. Their arrival

Linda Owen

Linda Owen

Above:
Cave near the site of Dieulacres Abbey, probably the
Chapel of the Virgin Mary at Cholpesdale referred to
in the Dieulacres Chronicle. M.J. Fisher argues that it
may have been an inhabited hermitage with associated
grotto chapel.

Right and below:
Details of the cave, showing evidence that at some
time it has been furnished with walls and doors.

Linda Owen

was resented by the monks of Croxden, since the new abbey would be closer to their house than the statutes of the order allowed (sixteen Burgundian leagues). The dispute was taken to the Chapter-General at Citeaux, and a settlement agreed which allowed building to continue. The abbey buildings were erected in an austere style then considered old-fashioned, perhaps to save money.

After the death of King John, Earl Ranulph went on Crusade to Egypt. On his return journey, the Chronicle records that a great storm blew up which terrified the crew. Ranulph remained calm throughout, and when, next day, the captain of the ship asked him for the secret of his composure, he replied that at that time his monks would be singing the night office. That had given him confidence that they would not be lost.

When Earl Ranulph was buried with his ancestors in the Benedictine Abbey at Chester, his heart was cut from his body and interred at Dieulacres according to his wishes. When his wife Clemencia died, in 1253, she was also buried at Dieulacres. According to the Chronicle, a blind monk who used to pray daily at her tomb miraculously recovered his sight.

When the earldom was absorbed by the Crown, the abbot of Dieulacres held Leek as tenant-in-chief, and the king became patron of the abbey. Dieulacres soon became the second largest monastic establishment in the county, the abbot sometimes being summoned to parliament. Indication of the style with which the abbots travelled the country can be gauged from the lease of Poulton Manor to a lay tenant in 1504, when it was stipulated that the lesee would have the obligation to provide hospitality for the abbot and twelve mounted companions for six days twice every

Linda Owen

One of two wheel windows in St Edward's Church, Leek, originally part of the now demolished Abbot's Chapel.

year. By the sixteenth century the abbey boasted thirty servants. Accordingly, the abbots of Dieulacres came to dominate the extreme north of the county. Sometimes this was to the benefit of the Town; sometimes they acted in a manner reminiscent of organised crime.

When the church and town of Leek accidentally burned down in the Great Fire of Leek of 10th June, 1297, abbot Robert Burgilon rebuilt the church in grand style. The most obvious indication of his flamboyance is the striking 'wheel windows', which M. J. Fisher calls: "a piece of extravagance ..... of the kind one would expect to see in the transept gables of an abbey or cathedral."

During the 1370s Abbot William Lichfield kept a band of armed retainers who were accused of repeated murders, maimings and assaults. They came to be involved in a feud with John Warton of Leek after he and his accomplices had attacked some of the abbey servants, injuring them so severely that the abbot was deprived of their services for some time. Led by two brothers, Henry and Richard Bradshaw, the abbot's retainers cornered Warton and shot at him, calling upon him to surrender, which he did. There are two versions of what happened next. According to one account, Warton was thrown into the Abbot's jail, and four days later taken to Leek Moor and summarily hanged by the Ashbourne Road. However Warton's wife testified that he had been killed almost immediately by being shot through the heart by Henry Bradshaw, although he had been so badly treated that any of his attackers might have delivered the fatal blow. The Abbot was accused of having ordered the murder. The court ordered the arrest of the Abbot, the Vicar of Leek, and all the others involved. The Abbot was thrown into the Marshalsea Prison, in London, but the others disappeared. After some time the abbot was released on bail. One by one the others involved gave themselves up, but only after each had acquired a document issued by the Crown pardoning them from all crimes committed before 14th December, 1381, as did the Abbot subsequently. As a result, they all escaped retribution.

During the fourteenth and fifteenth centuries the area around Leek frequently descended into lawlessness, and the abbots were as likely to find themselves the victims of violence as its perpetrators. William of Lichfield's successor, Abbot Richard of Whitmore, complained to the authorities several times about attacks upon his property and servants. For example, in 1413 he charged that five men had broken into his houses at Cheddleton, cutting down trees worth five pounds and threatening his servants so much that they were afraid to carry out their duties. Michael Fisher thinks that these were probably servants of William Egerton of Cheddleton, because of what seems like a revenge raid later that year. A band of men eighty-strong, some in armour and armed with swords and axes, and led by a monk, Nicholas of Poulton, went to Cheddleton 'in the manner of war', broke into the park of William Egerton and stole ironstone to the same value as the timber taken from the abbot's estate. Abbot Richard of Whitmore was accused of instigating the attack. Certainly the entire band afterwards went to the abbey, presumably to share out the spoils. The Abbot was charged with the others as an accessory, but a jury acquitted them.

An artist's idea of how Dieulacres Abbey may have looked.

His successor, Abbot John Goodfellow, became involved in a vicious vendetta between the Meverells of Throwley and the Bassetts of Blore which disturbed the north of the county during the 1440s, when the tithes of Throwley, which belonged to Ilam Church, were granted by John Southworth, the vicar, to Ralph Bassett. Sampson Meverell claimed that they should rightly have been his as lord of Throwley, and went to Ilam to make his point, taking with him about forty of his friends armed with swords, bows and arrows. The vicar refused to agree until, having been threatened with a violent death, he changed his mind and awarded them to Meverell. Basset refused to give up the tithes, and instigated a lawsuit. In response, in June 1448, Meverell, with thirteen armed men, including Abbot Whitmore and a priest from Grindon, paid a visit to Bassett's house at Blore, seriously injuring three of his servants and leaving with two dozen head of cattle.

In 1516, during a riot in Leek, a man named Paunsfote was murdered by servants of Sir John Savage, steward of the town. Abbot William Albion, John Savage and other abbey servants were accused of being involved, and William Egerton of Wall Grange was appointed to

Key found at the site of Dieulacres Abbey.

The seal of one of the abbots of Dieulacres Abbey.

Linda Owen

Linda Owen

Outbuildings at Abbey
Farm incorporating
fragments from
Dieulacres Abbey.

Left:
The base of one of the
central crossing piers of
the Abbey Church.

Linda Owen

Linda Owen

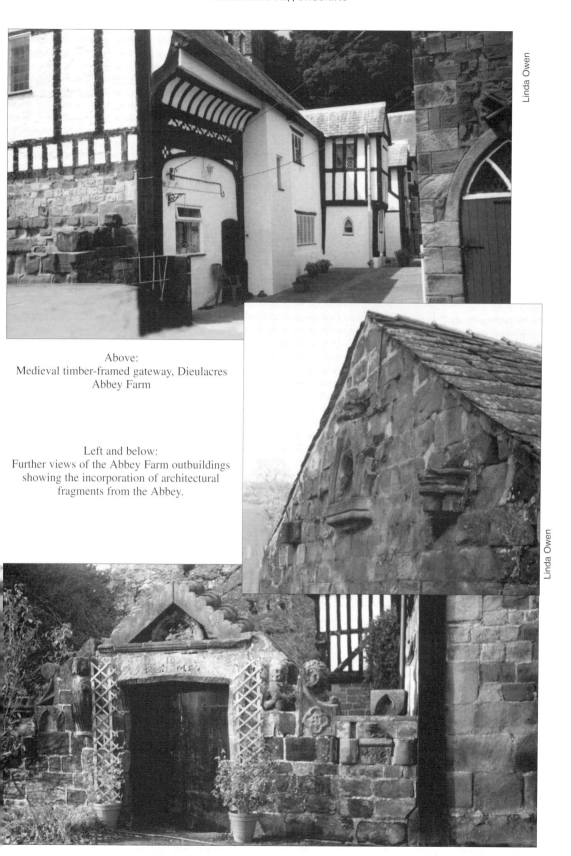

Above:
Medieval timber-framed gateway, Dieulacres
Abbey Farm

Left and below:
Further views of the Abbey Farm outbuildings
showing the incorporation of architectural
fragments from the Abbey.

Linda Owen

Linda Owen

investigate the matter. When he arrived to conduct his enquiries, a mob of abbey servants, tenants and their supporters some two hundred strong, led by John Brereton, chased him from house to house and cornered him in a tavern. While the mob waited outside the abbot and eight monks arrived on the scene. Brereton shot an arrow through the window, and the Abbot clearly considered doing so himself, for he was seen to 'take his bow from his monk, Whitney, and take an arrow from under his girdle and nick it into his bow'. Egerton and his friends only emerged when the crowd had got tired and gone away, and tried to slip unobtrusively out of the town. When they were spotted by Brereton and three of the abbot's brothers, they took refuge in St. Edward's Church. The abbot's servants built a barricade across the road, and would not allow anyone to take food to them for several days. The stand-off ended with Abbot Albion in the Fleet Gaol, in London.

He re-emerged around 1519 to hear that Brereton was virtually running the abbey, and that it had a bad reputation. Shocked by this, the by now apparently reformed abbot determined to put things right and institute some changes. This did not go down well with the monks or with Brereton, and they made serious allegations about him to the father abbot of Combermere, who visited Leek and deposed him.

His successor, Abbot John Wodeland, drew up a number of blank deeds, affixed to them the abbey seal, and then distributed them to his friends, so that they could write grants of whatever they liked on them from the Abbey's resources. He was deposed in 1523.

The last abbot of Dieulacres, Thomas Whitney, made efforts to set the Abbey's finances right. He tried to recover the blank deeds, but was only partially successful. Some of the means he chose to restore the Abbey's finances were dubious, to say the least. He found it necessary to resort to violence against Abbey tenants on several occasions, assaulting the tenants themselves, breaking down their hedges and taking their livestock. What this could mean for individuals can be seen in the case of a young tenant of Easing Farm. Shortly after Abbot Whitney leased the farm, the lesee died, leaving a thirteen-year-old grandson, Richard Mounford. The Abbot was asked by the family to lease the farm to him, which he promised to do for twelve years following the death or re-marriage of his grandmother. When his grandmother remarried, in 1527, the boy should have taken over the farm, but his uncle took it over instead with the Abbot's support, drawing the income from it. When Richard reached the age of twenty-one and decided to stand up for his rights, the Abbot told his uncle to throw him out. They assaulted him, threw his belongings outside, demolished the cottage he was living in, and then the Abbot falsely accused him in court of forcibly entering the premises. Homeless, he was in no position to defend himself. Fortunately, friends brought the matter to the attention of the Court of Star Chamber, although the result is not known.

In 1530, when there was a disagreement over some land in Cheddleton, an armed band, including Abbot Whitney, went to evict John Massey, one of the tenants there. They threw his children out of the window of his house, and drove away his livestock.

Pages 97-99:
Further views showing the incorporation of architectural fragments from the Abbey

Linda Owen

Linda Owen

Linda Owen

Linda Owen

Linda Owen

The Mysteries of the Green Chapel and the Green Knight

The Abbey of Dieulacres has a close but elusive connection with four famous medieval works of literature, the oldest copies of which are preserved in a single manuscript: Sir Gawain and the Green Knight, Pearl, Patience, and Purity. Of these, the story of Sir Gawain and the Green Knight is most celebrated.

This romantic Arthurian tale opens when a huge Green Knight burst into King Arthur's court at Camelot (Caerleon-on-Usk) during the New Year celebrations. This terrifying and mysterious figure challenged the assembled knights to strike off his head with an axe, on condition that the one who dealt the blow must present himself for a return blow a year and a day afterwards at a mysterious green chapel. Only Gawain had the courage to meet the challenge. He struck off the Green Knight's head with a single blow, only to see the stranger pick up his severed head, mount his horse and ride out of the palace chuckling.

At the beginning of the following winter, Gawain rode out from Arthur's court to keep his appointment at the Green Chapel. He travelled for some weeks through the dying winter landscape until, just before Christmas, he emerged from the frozen forest lowlands and came upon a castle in the 'Hautdesert' or High Forest. There he was welcomed by Sir Bertilak and his wife in his castle, and entertained until the day of his appointment, his host assuring him that the Green Chapel he sought was close by.

During his stay, Gawain and Bertilak make an agreement that Bertilak would hunt during the day while his guest would rest in the castle, and in the evening they would exchange their winnings. While her husband was out hunting, Bertilak's wife made determined attempts to seduce Gawain. On the first two days she managed only to get him to accept kisses from her, but on the third, she persuaded him to accept three kisses and a magic garter or belt which would keep him safe.

On the next morning, Gawain rode to meet the Green Knight at the Green Chapel. Three blows were delivered by the Knight against Gawain, but he survived. The Green Knight then revealed his true identity and mission, and insisted that Gawain keep the belt and take it back with him to Camelot.

It is clear to scholars that the poet wrote during the 1380-90s, during the reign of King Richard II, although using an archaic style employing the Old English rhythmic and alliterative poetic metre instead of the more modern rhyming form introduced by the Normans. In alliterative verse, each line is divided into two half lines with a rhythmic break between them, and the unity between the half lines is established by the poet's choosing words which begin with the same sounds.

The central point of the story concerns the three temptations undergone by Gawain in Sir Bertilak's castle, and this presupposes a sophisticated understanding of contemporary codes of chivalry, which could only have been intended for a cultured and sophisticated audience. Yet the poet wrote in a dialect spoken only in south-east Cheshire and north Staffordshire, and so presumably for a local audience. Naturally, there has been much discussion about where such an audience could have been found in this area. There is really only one possibility: that it was written for the

Linda Owen

Ludchurch

court of John of Gaunt, Duke of Lancaster and son of Edward III. The most powerful noble of his age, he held extensive lands in this area at just the time that the poem was written, and he maintained a court in his castles of Newcastle-under-Lyme, Chartley, Tutbury, and others. It is most likely that as highly cultured a court as his would have required entertainment, particularly during the winter months.

A careful reading of the detailed itinerary of Sir Gawain's travels by Professor Ralph Elliott traces his route northwards from Caerleon, through the borderlands of Wales, across the River Dee, across the plain of Cheshire along the Earlsway, into precisely that area in the dialect of which the poem is written. Based on evidence within the poem itself, Professor Elliot has argued that the site of the Green Chapel, described as half cave, half crevice, is the natural chasm known as Lud Church, situated in the upper reaches of the Dane Valley, on the estate of Dieulacres Abbey. The element Lud appears in the names Lludebroc and Lludebeche in the charter by which Earl Ranulph gave lands near Leek to the monks on their transfer from Poulton.

It is impossible here to reproduce the extremely detailed and persuasive reasoning by which this identification is established, but this 'weird, legend-haunted natural 'chapel' in the Staffordshire moorlands' lies just two miles from a hill in an enclosed park (Swythamley Grange), in the 'Hautdesert' or High Forest of the Pennines, just as the poem requires.

Because of the religious tone of the poem, and even more because of the character of the poet's other works, it is usually argued that he was probably a priest or monk. The last part of Sir Gawain's journey follows the route the monks of Dieulacres would have taken in leaving their original home at Poulton for their new home at Leek. It is hardly surprising, therefore, that David Clarke, in his *Guide to Britain's Pagan Heritage*,

Ludchurch. The 'top' entrance.

suggests that the Gawain poet may have been a monk of Dieulacres Abbey. Certainly, Michael Fisher shows from his investigation of the Dieulacres Chronicle that some of the monks must have been extremely well-read.

The Green Knight seems to be connected with a familiar but strange figure often seen in medieval carving known as the Green Man. This bizarre image of a severed male human head with leaves and foliage intertwined around it, often sprouting from the mouth and nostrils, is found carved upon roof bosses, capitals, rood screens and misericords in medieval churches. It has been thought to represent a pagan fertility spirit. The oldest date from the Norman Conquest, but there was a great upsurge during the fourteenth and fifteenth centuries, which coincides with the writing of Sir Gawain.

Kathleen Basford, who published the first academic study of the Green Man, was amazed to see an example in the ruins of Fountains abbey, in Yorkshire. This was striking because carving was usually avoided on Cistercian buildings. A representation of the Green Man, dating from the early fifteenth century also appears on the choir stalls of St Mary's Church, Nantwich, which local tradition says came from the Abbey of Combermere. Early in the nineteenth century a carving of a green man was discovered on the site of Dieulacres Abbey itself.

Seven carved bosses depicting the Green Man appear in the Lady Chapel of Sheffield Cathedral, where a set of carvings on the wooden roof, decorated with gold paint, dating from the fifteenth-century, appear to have pagan religious significance. In 1939, Lady Raglan, who gave the figure its name, suggested a connection with pagan ritual festivals, and identified the Green Man with the figure who danced, adorned in foliage, in many rural May Day processions, and who, in the village of Castleton, in Derbyshire, was paraded on horseback covered in a garland of leaves and flowers. Another related figure is Jack in the Green, who danced ahead of the May Queen in May Day processions, such as those at Knutsford. The Green Man may also be associated with the mythological aspects of the Robin Hood legend.

Linda Owen

Medieval Green Man. Left: Panel in Daresbury Church, Derbyshire.
Right: 'Green Man' on Nantwich Parish Church choir stalls which probably came from Combermere Abbey.

A "Green Man" roof
boss in the Nantwich
Parish Church.

The Green Knight at the Court
of King Arthur.

Hulton Abbey

The founder of a third daughter house of Combermere, this time at Abbey Hulton, in Staffordshire, was Henry of Audley, probably head of a branch of the Verdun family. Henry inherited and acquired lands in north Staffordshire, and became an important supporter of Earl Ranulph de Blundeville of Chester during the latter years of the reign of King John.

On Ash Wednesday in 1216, the King, Earl Ranulph and a great host of their followers made a solemn vow to go on crusade. The performance of their vow was delayed when, in October of that year, the King died, leaving the country in a state of civil war. After a delegation of Cistercian abbots from France had arranged a peace treaty in May 1218, Earl Ranulph was able to leave for the siege of Damietta, in Egypt, leaving Henry behind as sheriff of Staffordshire and Shropshire. It is likely that the

The seal of the Abbey of Hulton.

foundation of Hulton Abbey was in part Henry's substitute for his broken vow, as well as thanksgiving for a socially advantageous marriage he had recently contracted.

Monks at Combermere were chosen to go to Hulton in 1218 or 1219. In 1220 Abbot Thomas of Woodstock of Croxden was complaining once more to the Chapter-General of the building of yet another daughter house of Combermere within a prohibited distance from his house. Once more the Chapter-General ordered the building at Hulton to be suspended pending the report of a special commission. A verdict in favour of the new community was evidently reached, for in 1222 the 'foundation' of Hulton Abbey was recorded in the Croxden Chronicle. The buildings erected at Hulton were, like those at Dieulacres, of unusually conservative character, and since building was still going on at Leek when it began at Hulton, there was probably some sharing of expertise.

The original endowment of this house consisted of two manors: Hulton, covering Abbey Hulton, Sneyd Green and Cobridge; and Normacot, containing what is now Meir Heath. This was supplemented by additional smaller grants of land in Bucknall by other benefactors. This was not a generous endowment, and in 1232 on the death of Earl Ranulph, the founder added the manor of Mixon and Bradnop, outside Leek, on condition that 'during all the days of the world remaining' thirteen monks would celebrate mass daily for the soul of Earl Ranulf, the founder, and the members of his family.

As we have already seen, during 1264, during the upheaval of the Barons' Wars, the men of Stone Priory attacked and looted Hulton's estate at Normacot. The impression of prevailing lawlessness is reinforced when we learn that in 1268 the abbot of Hulton, while on his way to Stafford to pursue a writ in the King's Court, was kidnapped by Walter of Hopton and John of Bromeshull, and held until a ransom of two pounds had been paid. The extent of this lawlessness is evident in that Walter of Hopton had been sheriff of the county during the previous year, and his kidnapping of the abbot proved no barrier to his reappointment as sheriff in 1277.

The history of Hulton Abbey demonstrates the great difficulties a small house might experience simply in securing control of gifts made to them by their patrons. Just before the Black Death, James II of Audley gave to the monks the rectory of Marwood, in Devon. The men of Hulton went to considerable trouble and expense to obtain the proper royal licence then necessary to secure their legal claim to the income of this church, including payments to lawyers and to the Crown. Unfortunately, Marwood church was not James's to give. He only held it for the duration of the lives of himself and his wife, after which it was to go to his brother. Thus the men of Hulton had to face the unpleasant realisation that the gift which they had gone to so much considerable trouble and expense to secure was lost to them.

Following the Black Death, and perhaps in compensation for his previous error, James gave them Audley Church. On this occasion no attempt was made by the monks to comply with the law. They had already gone to the trouble and expense of obtaining a licence for Marwood, and they probably felt that, having unnecessarily paid once, they should not have to pay a second time. It may also be that they were distracted by the plague. Their lapse was detected, and a fine of two hundred marks was imposed on the house in return for allowing the gift to stand. In 1351 the fine was halved since the Abbey was 'impoverished'.

Even then it was not until more than thirty years had passed that the monks were able to gain undisputed possession of this gift. Because of the confusion over the license, and the plague, William Whittlesey, archbishop of Canterbury, supported by the bishop of Lichfield, was able to claim the church on the basis of a legal technicality. Lord James responded in an energetic and robust fashion. Contrary to the evidence of all surviving records, he denied that he had ever made the bequest in the first place, and then launched a series of writs against the bishop for impeding his rights to it, claiming substantial damages. The case dragged on until 1373, when he had the proceedings moved to Newcastle-under-Lyme and the jury found in his favour. When Archbishop Whittlesey was dead, the abbot of Hulton was finally able to appropriate the income of the church.

Further attempts to reinforce the economic base of the monastery were made during the last decades of the century by Nicholas and his widow, Elizabeth. Nicholas donated the church of Biddulph. Since the priest's house had burned down and they paid the vicar very little, there were problems in getting a priest to stay there for any length of time.

In 1396, Hulton Abbey acquired the lands and property of the small alien Priory of Cammeringham, eight miles north of Lincoln. In June 1395, Elizabeth, Nicholas's widow, paid £100 to the Crown for it, but enjoyment by the men of Hulton of this new source of income was interrupted almost immediately. In 1398 the estate was seized by Thomas of Holland, Earl of Kent and Duke of Surrey, a nephew and favourite of Richard II. The case was taken to court at Lincoln and the jury found in the abbot's favour, awarding him damages of £20. Mere verdict of the court might not have settled the issue in face of so powerful an opponent, but after Edward IV seized the throne, Thomas became implicated in a plot to rescue the deposed King Richard and restore him to power. He was seized by a mob at Salisbury and beheaded. Cammeringham became the Abbey's most profitable estate.

Granges were set up at Hulton, Rushton and Normacot. Hulton Abbey kept sheep at Mixon and Normacot and probably sold their wool in London, for, in 1389, the abbot was sued for a debt of £112 by John Donnington, a London draper. Like many other houses, they had fallen into the trap of selling their wool crop in advance. The abbey organised extensive clearing of land, especially on the slopes of Morridge.

Fish were farmed, involving considerable manipulation of the waters of the Trent, and of the streams flowing into it from Wetley Moor to the north and south of the abbey site. Shallow rectangular pan-shaped depressions cut into the meadow between the Abbey and the Trent were still visible as late as the 1970s.

The industrial future of the area may be detected in some of the activities of the monks, despite the fact that there is no evidence that they engaged in the manufacture of pottery. There was a tannery near the abbey site, while a fulling mill existed on the Trent to the south-west of the abbey corn mill for some time.

The practice of mining coal in North Staffordshire had already begun before the end of the thirteenth century, although initially it was limited to areas where the coal seams outcropped. By the early years of the sixteenth century, at the very latest, coal was mined on the estates of Hulton Abbey. A coal mine leased to Thomas Fox was probably situated in the area of Milton later known as Foxley. Coal was used for industrial rather than domestic purposes at that time, and the mine was not used to supply the Abbey with coal; the rent received for it was used to maintain the hospice for visitors.

Hulton Abbey was also associated with the working of iron during this period, when the abbot got into a dispute with Christopher Edge and others over the lease of a bloomsmithy at Horton Hay. Both claimed to have been in lawful occupation, and each was forcibly thrown out by the other at different times. In the process, smith wheels were broken, charcoal burned away, tools destroyed, the blow hearth and even the walls of the smithy cast down. The court testimony suggests that in addition to smelting the ore, the metal was worked at the site using a water-driven hammer forge, a method pioneered by the Cistercians.

From 1405, Hulton Abbey engaged in commercial activity in Newcastle-under-

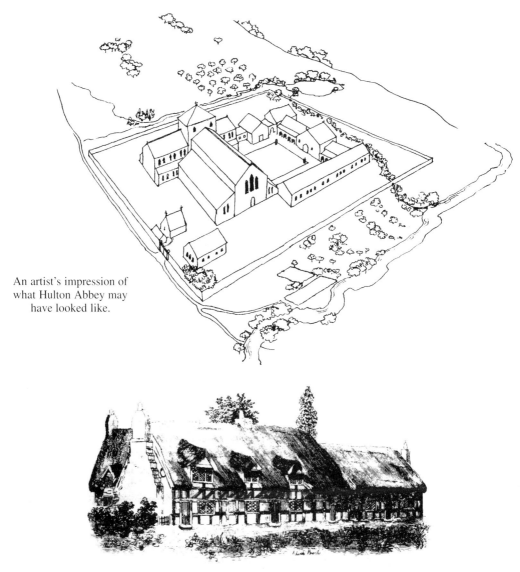

An artist's impression of
what Hulton Abbey may
have looked like.

Rushton Grange. Engraving in Ward's *History of the Borough of Stoke upon Trent*, 1843.

A 19th century illustration of Abbey Mill, formerly the grist mill for the abbey and their tenants.

The Potteries Museum

Aerial view of the site of Hulton Abbey, showing the outline of a series of rectangular ponds used for fish-farming. The site of the abbey buildings is at the top of the photo next to the school.

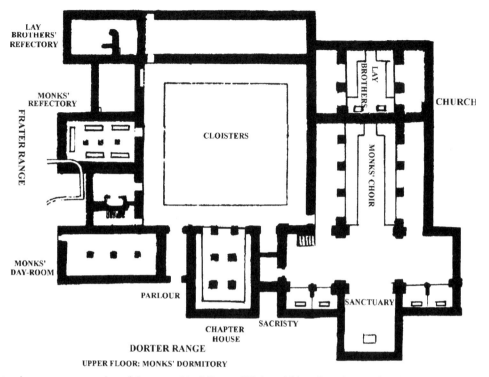

CELLARER'S RANGE

LOWER FLOOR: STORES AND LAY BROTHERS' FACILITIES   UPPER FLOOR: LAY BROTHERS' DORMITORY

LAY BROTHERS' REFECTORY

MONKS' REFECTORY

FRATER RANGE

CLOISTERS

LAY BROTHERS

CHURCH

MONKS' CHOIR

MONKS' DAY-ROOM

PARLOUR

CHAPTER HOUSE

SACRISTY

SANCTUARY

DORTER RANGE

UPPER FLOOR: MONKS' DORMITORY

A Cistercian monastery: a plan of the central buildings of Hulton Abbey, based upon the plan of C. Lynam, in "Hulton Abbey" - *Transactions of North Staffs Field Club* XIX 1885. The plan has been adjusted in the light of recently published archaeological work on the east end of the church. (The Potteries Museum)

Gravestones removed from the site of Hulton Abbey.

(The Potteries Museum)

Lyme, being exempt from local tolls, and possessed a tenement in the High Street, adjoining the Antelope Inn. The monks may have been selling cloth from their fulling mill, and were perhaps planning to sell products in the iron market. In 1407, Abbot Richard Billington was leasing two salt pans at Northwich to Sir Richard Whittington, the 'Dick Whittington' of pantomime fame. The increasing participation of the Abbey in the money economy made recourse to bankers a necessity. Hulton Abbey banked with the Abbey of Oseney, an important house of Augustinian canons in the western suburbs of Oxford, which acted in this way for many religious houses.

Like all the monks, the men of Hulton soon began leasing their lands for money rents. At the beginning of the sixteenth century Thomas Rode of Congleton claimed that certain lands and tenements had been in the hands of his family for more than a hundred years. He accused the abbot's bailiff and his servants of seriously wounding some of the abbey tenants and stealing their cattle. It may be that the monks found themselves in receipt of rents which had been agreed upon many years previously on long term leases and which had lost their value due to inflation, and were attempting either to extract some compensation for their 'losses' or simply to force the tenants out.

Hulton saw its share of internal dissension. In 1344 when the Father Abbot, Roger Lyndley of Combermere, made his formal visitation, as he was leaving the Abbey precincts with the abbot of Whalley and their households, they were attacked by a band of armed men led by Thomas of Keele, described as a 'renegade monk of Hulton'. A priest in one of the abbots' retinues was gravely wounded before they regained the safety of the enclosure walls. For ten days the visitors were besieged until forced to surrender, when they were obliged to agree to the deposition of the abbot of Hulton and the election of another member of the community in his place. The matter was discussed at Citeaux and the abbot of Savigny entrusted with the suppression of the revolt and the imposition of good order.

On a subsequent occasion, a breach of discipline involved the abbot himself. In 1416, Sampson Meverell sued Abbot Richard Billington for abducting his servant, Joan Condale, by force while she was in his service at Hulton. The Abbot failed to appear in court and the sheriff was ordered to arrest him.

After the extinction of the direct male line of the Audleys, patronage of Hulton passed to the Talbots, earls of Shrewsbury. Hulton lies between the Talbot estates in Yorkshire and Derbyshire to the north and east, and those in Shropshire, Herefordshire and Gloucestershire to the south and west, and may have served them as a hostelry for estate officials and servants travelling from one set of estates to another.

In 1535 the community at Hulton found itself deprived of a head when Abbot John Hareware moved to Vale Royal, in Cheshire, to become abbot of that house. On August 28th the patron of Hulton, the Earl of Shrewsbury, wrote to Thomas Cromwell to inform him that the monks of Hulton wished to elect William Chawner to replace him, 'as well for his good and virtuous living as also for his politic wisdom'. However, on the very next day, Sir Philip Draycot, steward of the abbey, wrote to point out that the abbot of Croxden had been pushing the cause of his own brother: 'Upon the said abbot's report, he is a good monk, where of truth he is very vicious and drunken'. He warned Cromwell that any letter bearing the abbey seal in favour of this monk would be against the wishes of the two wisest priests in the house. In his own opinion, every monk then at Hulton was 'too young or too old or too mad' to become abbot. Cromwell evidently took his advice, for an outsider, Edward Wilkins, was appointed.

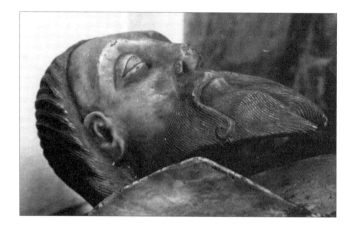

Tomb of Sir William Draycot, last Steward of Hulton Abbey, in Draycot Parish Church.

Items recovered from excavations on the site of Hulton Abbey. Pages 113-115

The Potteries Museum

Above: Gilded stars probably used to decorate a chest, book or belt.

Left: Corbel from the chancel.

Below: Ceramic pedestal for salt.

The Potteries Museum

The Potteries Museum

Left:
Chess piece of red jasper stone,
probably a rook.

Below:
Troy weights, 2oz and 1oz.

The Potteries Museum

Three handled cup.

The Potteries Museum

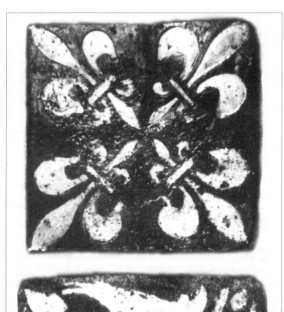

The Potteries Museum

The Potteries Museum

Above: Belt hook, late 15th century

Left: Medieval floor tiles from the chancel

Below:
Fragment of window glass. The glass was originally greenish in colour, decorated with a reddish-brown paint, which would have appeared as black when the glass was in place.

The Potteries Museum

the crusades

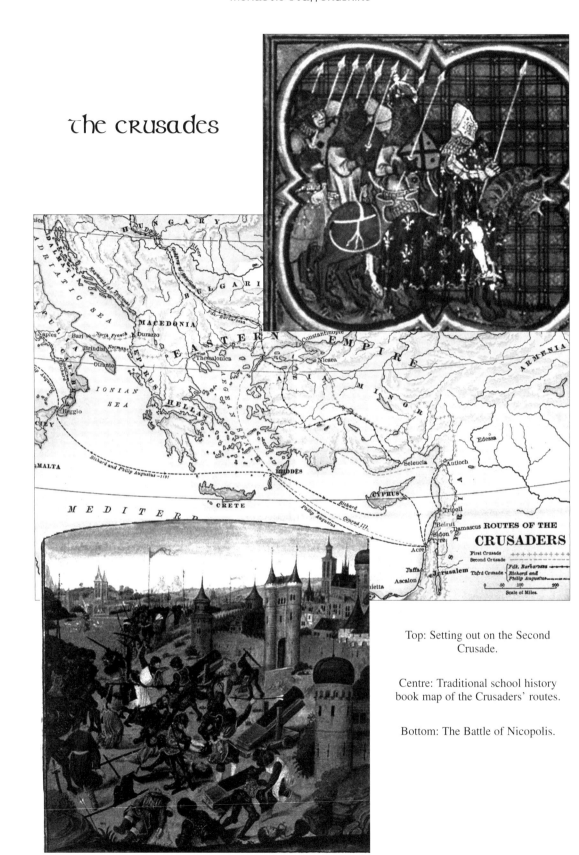

Top: Setting out on the Second Crusade.

Centre: Traditional school history book map of the Crusaders' routes.

Bottom: The Battle of Nicopolis.

chapter five
the soldier monks

A strange offshoot of the Crusades and the monastic reform movement which had created the Cistercians was the emergence of religious orders dedicated to warfare.

The Knights Templar

The Knights Templar, or Poor Knights of Christ and of the Temple of Solomon, first appeared when the crusaders had come to control strongholds in the Holy Land, but when pilgrims to the holy places were still frequently endangered by marauding bands of hostile Muslims. A small group of French knights, led by Hugues de Payens, vowed, at sometime between 1114 and 1118, to devote themselves to their protection and formed a religious community for that purpose. Baldwin II, King of Jerusalem, gave them a wing of the royal palace, Solomon's Stables in the area of the former Jewish Temple, as their headquarters. From this location the Templars took their name.

Jerusalem at night. The temple is on the far right; the temple stables on the far left.

St. Bernard of Clairvaux wrote a rule of life for them, based upon that of the Cistercians. Each individual Templar took vows of poverty and chastity, yet they had to be prepared to defend the Christian possessions in the Holy Land against attack. They were, as Desmond Seward put it: 'Monks, booted and spurred, carrying swords'. According to Saint Bernard there was no contradiction in this, since 'to kill a pagan is to win glory, since it gives glory to Christ'.

Two Contemporary illustrations of Templar knights.

Each branch of the order was headed by a commander under the grand master of the order. The members were divided into four classes: knights, sergeants, chaplains, and servants. The knights wore the distinctive regalia of a white surcoat marked with a red cross patée. At their height, there were about twenty thousand knights. Kings and great nobles gave them castles and estates, so that by the mid-twelfth century the Templars were a wealthy order, owning properties throughout Western Europe, the Mediterranean, and the Holy Land.

The Preceptory of Keele

Towards the end of the 1160s, Henry II gave Keele to the Templars, and by 1185 he had added lands in Madeley and Onneley. There were advantages in working for the Templars. All tenants, labourers and even domestic servants of the order had the right to mark their houses with a Templar cross exempting them from various controls and taxes. Moreover, the Templars had the reputation of being less oppressive landlords than the other religious orders. Their demands for labour service were lighter; and tenants were free to inherit, sell, lease, divide or mortgage their tenancies at will. Dr Robin Studd of Keele University considers that this would have led to an influx of settlers eager to escape the normal obligations and restrictions of feudal society.

At first the Keele estate was merely leased for rent, but during the thirteenth century it was upgraded and became a preceptory, with Templars in residence. Probably only one or two would ever have actually lived at Keele, where they would have been lodged in a hall next to the church. By 1308 the preceptory also enjoyed rents in Newcastle-under-Lyme, Stanton (in Shropshire), and Nantwich.

The Templars established the first international banking service. Travellers not wishing to make long journeys carrying large sums of money could deposit their cash at any Temple and be refunded at their destination. Their military strength, network of secure vaults and efficient transport organisation enabled them to store and transport bullion to and from Europe and the Holy Land. They offered a full range of financial services to kings, including the collection of taxes, and the administration of debts and pension funds.

This wealth inevitably made them enemies. They engaged in bitter rivalry with another great military order, the Hospitallers, and by the late thirteenth century proposals were being made to merge these two orders into one. The fall to the Muslims in 1291 of the last remaining crusader stronghold in the Holy Land, seemed to remove much of the Templars' reason for existence. Moreover, by 1304 dark rumours had begun to circulate of secret initiation rites during which blasphemous and irreligious practices were enacted.

In 1306 Philip 'the Handsome' of France was forced to take refuge inside the Paris headquarters of the Templars to avoid a hostile mob. What he saw there aroused his cupidity. He had already seized the property of the Jews, squeezed forced loans out of the Lombard bankers, and 'borrowed' money from the Templars for a dowry for his daughter, Isabella, popularly known as the 'she-wolf of France'. Philip's chancellor, Guillaume de Nogaret, a lawyer whose parents had been burned at the stake as heretics, set to work for the King to build a case against the Templars by sending secret agents to join the Order.

On the night of Thursday 12th October

Seal of the Templar Knights showing the Church of the Holy Sepulchre in Jerusalem, which they were sworn to defend.

Seal of the Knights Templar. The two riders share a horse as a symbol of the poverty supposedly chosen by the knights as a part of their religious vocation.

Shield of the Knights Templar.

Templars, showing a knight, priest and sergeant.

1307, without any warning, Philip's soldiers arrested Jacques de Molay, the Grand Master, and fifteen thousand other Templars across France, charging them with denying Christ, worshipping idols, spitting on the crucifix and homosexuality. In order to establish guilt by confession, torture was used systematically. Many died during the process of interrogation and a few confessed to absurd crimes.

At first the Pope protested, but after reading some of the confessions he changed his mind and ordered the arrest of all the Templars throughout Christendom. In most countries these orders were followed reluctantly, and those arrested soon declared, after investigation, to be innocent. In England the pope had more influence, and was able to insist upon the use of torture, so that more incriminating confessions were obtained.

In 1310 most of the imprisoned brothers in France retracted their confessions. Royal agents were sent out to spread stories that the Templars slept with female fiends, worshipped cats, roasted children in front of idols, and so on. After a show trial those Templars who had not retracted their confessions were released to live as beggars, while the others were sentenced to be burned at the stake. The Pope formally suppressed the order on March 22nd 1312, and the Templars' property throughout Europe was transferred to the rival military order of the Hospitallers.

On 14th March 1314, the

The burning of the Grand Master of the Templars in Paris.

highest officers of the Order were paraded on a platform in front of Notre-Dame in Paris. Jacques de Molay seized the occasion publicly to affirm his innocence of all the charges levelled against him, claiming that he had only confessed to save himself from the terrible torture. For this he was roasted alive over a slow charcoal fire. Before all the people, he cursed Pope and King, summoning both to appear before God's judgement seat. The Pope was dead within a month, the King within a year, and all the King's immediate successors died young. The guilt or innocence of the Templars has been a matter of controversy for centuries, but modern historians are generally of the opinion that they were victims of a highly unjust, opportunistic but well-organised persecution.

With the seizure of the property of the Templars in England on 20th January, 1308, the Keele estate passed into the hands of the Crown. The Preceptor of Keele, Ralph Taret, the only member of the order in residence, was 'interrogated' with seven others at Bishop's House, near Saint Paul's Cathedral, in London. Under torture they confessed that they had denied Christ at their reception into the order, that they had spat upon the cross, and various other misdeeds. These acts they abjured, and were given absolution lying prostrate on the steps before the west door of Saint Paul's Cathedral. They were then given penances to perform.

Keele was secured in 1314 by Thomas, Earl of Lancaster. When he was executed in 1322, it reverted to the Crown. In 1324 it was finally given to the rival Hospitallers. Instead of establishing a preceptory of their own at Keele, they simply attached the estate to their Commandery of Halston, in Shropshire.

The Siege of Damietta
(1218-1219)
Earl Ranulph de Blundeville of Chester made the journey to Egypt with a host of his followers after supervising the establishment of his monastery of Dieulacres at Leek. (see p. 105)
While he was in Egypt, Saint Assisi also arrived in an attempt to convert the Sultan, the Saracen leader, to Christianity.

The Knights Hospitaller

The origin of the Knights of the Hospital of Saint John lay in an eleventh century hospital in Jerusalem founded by Italian merchants from Amalfi to care for sick pilgrims. After the conquest of Jerusalem in the First Crusade, Gerard, the hospital's superior, founded hostels in Provencal and Italian cities on routes to the Holy Land.

The grand master ruled a brotherhood of knights, chaplains, and serving brothers distinguished by a white cross on their black cloaks, who combined the task of tending the sick with waging war on Islam. Along with the Templars, they became the most formidable military order in the Holy Land and acquired similar wealth.

When the Muslims recaptured Jerusalem in 1187, the Hospitallers removed their headquarters to Acre, to Cyprus, and then to Rhodes, which they came to rule as an independent state. For more than two centuries the Knights of Rhodes were the scourge of Muslim shipping in the eastern Mediterranean.

The Preceptory of Yeaveley and Barrow

At some time during the reign of Richard I, Ralph Foun gave a hermitage at Yeaveley, in Shirley, Derbyshire, to the Hospitallers on condition that they should take him in if he should wish to join, and that the existing tenant of the hermitage should act as steward of the estate. The preceptory was dedicated to Saint Mary and Saint John the Baptist in 1268, and received extra donations from several people, including William Meynell. The Hospitallers later acquired lands in Compton in Ashbourne, and Barrow. In 1338 there were two brothers in residence.

Like the Templars, the Hospitallers were popular landlords, whose tenants enjoyed considerable privileges. In 1276 the townspeople of Ashbourne complained that the Knights were increasing the number of their tenants because of these, especially on account of their freedom from trading and bridge tolls. The Knights had also acquired the right to inspect and certify the gallon and bushel measures which previously had been checked by officers of the town, and it was alleged that they were allowing their tenants to sell bread and beer using false measures. These charges may have been true for when, in 1330, a sheriff's officer arrived at Barrow to examine the weights and measures, the brothers refused him entrance.

By the sixteenth century the estate was leased to the Babington family of Lea. Since in 1516 the preceptor was John Babington, and the lease was to his father, Thomas, there was clearly a family interest in the estate. In 1535 the preceptor, Sir Andrew Cove, was living in the manor house.

Two images of Hospitaller Knights
from a triptych on the High Altar of
St John's, Vienna.

The Palace of the Grand Master, Rhodes, the central headquarters of the order from 1309 to 1523.

The profits of the Hospitaller estates in Western Europe went to support fortresses like Krak des Chevaliers in Syria. In 1142 Count Raymond of Tripoli gave it to the Hospitallers. It successfully resisted attacks in 1163 and 1164, and again in 1188 by Salâh al-Dîn. It finally fell to Mamlûk Sultan Baybars in 1271 after a siege.

Left: The Church of Yeaveley Preceptory p126

Linda Owen

Right and below: Styd Hall, built on the site of the Hospitallers' Preceptory.

Linda Owen

Linda Owen

Walls of the Church of Yeaveley
Preceptory.
They were incorrectly re-erected in 1915
with the inside of the wall facing outwards.

Linda Owen

The Church of Yeaveley Preceptory
showing architectural detail.

Right: Baptismal Font.

Linda Owen

Linda Owen

Linda Owen

A Travelling Friar.

chapter six
the friars

Early in the thirteenth century it came to be thought that the existing religious orders were too far removed from the life of the people, and that more active movements were needed for evangelisation, particularly in the new towns which were springing up all over Europe.

The Grey Friars

The Franciscans were founded in the early thirteenth century by St. Francis of Assisi, who felt the call to a life of total poverty. In 1209 he and eleven of his followers journeyed to Rome where they received approval of their rule from Pope Innocent III.

Initially, the friars could own no possessions of any kind, either individually or communally. They wandered and preached among the people, helping the poor and the sick, supporting themselves by working and by begging food, but were forbidden to accept money either as payment for work or as alms. The impact of these street preachers, and especially of their founder, was immense, so that within ten years they numbered some five thousand.

From the fresco in the Basilica of Saint
Francis, Assisi.
Above: Saint Francis.
Right: Saint Francis preaching to the birds.

Even before the death of Francis, in 1226, conflicts had begun to develop within the order over the ideal of total poverty. Rapid expansion created a need for permanent houses, but it was impossible to justify these if Francis's rule was followed strictly. Three parties gradually differentiated themselves: the Zealots, who insisted on a literal observance of the primitive rule, including communal as well as personal poverty; the Moderates, who wanted communal (but not individual) possessions, and the Laxists, who favoured many mitigations of the rule. A compromise was reached between these different schools of thought when St. Bonaventure was minister general (1257-74).

The Franciscans arrived in England as early as 1224, initially settling in Canterbury, London and Oxford. The friaries which were set up in Staffordshire were all under the supervision of the priory of Worcester.

Lichfield Priory

Tradition attributes the foundation of the first friary in Staffordshire to Bishop Alexander Stavensby (1224-38). The buildings were under construction in 1237 when King Henry III assigned thirty oak trees in Cannock Forest for the work. Periodically grants of money were made by the king in their support.

This work came to nothing in 1291 with the Great Fire of Lichfield, when the new buildings were burned down in common with most of the town. The plight of the Lichfield Franciscans aroused sympathy among other members of their order. When, in 1294, they won a court case against Westminster Abbey and were awarded sixty marks, part of it was assigned to the rebuilding of Lichfield Priory.

The popularity of the Franciscans at this time is attested by many small bequests, but that sentiment was not universal. In 1338, friars from Lichfield were set upon while travelling to Worcester. A novice was stripped of his habit and forcibly dressed in lay clothing, suggesting considerable hostility in some quarters.

Their populism could sometimes enrage the church authorities. In 1531 one of the friars preached a sermon attacking church taxes and fees. He and the warden of the house had to appear before the chapter of the cathedral to apologise. Hoping to discourage people from attending the friars' church, the chapter ordered the seats for the people to be taken out.

A friar at prayer.

Stafford Franciscan Priory

The existence of Franciscan friars at Stafford is first known of in 1274. Initially there seems to have been some opposition to them here also, for it was reported that town officials would 'snatch what they had bought out of their hands'. In 1282 they had to obtain a license to 'buy without molestation of the king's ministers'. An early sign of acceptance was when Baron Edmund of Stafford appointed a Franciscan as his personal confessor, and chose to be buried in the Franciscan church rather than with his ancestors in Stone Priory.

Franciscan friars were usually in origin from a lower social class than the enclosed monks and nuns or the canons. Although many of the friars at Stafford were recruited locally, a surprising number are known to have been Welshmen. The Franciscans of Stafford were one of the few communities of their order which engaged in agriculture, working six strips in one of the common fields outside the town.

The tomb of Saint Francis, Assisi.

The Black Friars

The Black Friars, or members of the order of Friars Preachers, were founded by St. Dominic in 1215. A Spanish priest, he was accompanying his bishop on a preaching mission among the Albigensian heretics of southern France, where he had the idea of an order of preachers which would convert heretics by the force of argument.

Dominic set up his first community at Toulouse, in Southern France. In contrast to the monastic orders, the Dominican order was not a collection of autonomous communities. The individual belonged to the order, and could be sent anywhere at any time. The friars were also obliged to study in order to preach effectively. In southern France they preached against the Albigensians, in Spain against the Moors, and everywhere against the Jews. When the Inquisition was established to root out and extirpate heresy, the Dominicans were entrusted with its execution. They were

Saint Dominic,
and below, Dominican Friars from
a manuscript in the Vatican Library.

also heavily involved in the development of universities. Within forty years of the foundation of the order, Dominican friars were to be found at the universities at Oxford, Cambridge Paris, Bologna, and Cologne. Some of the greatest thinkers of the Middle Ages belonged to this order.

Newcastle-under-Lyme Priory

The Dominicans arrived in England in the middle of the thirteenth century, and established some sixty houses. It is not known when they arrived in Newcastle-under-Lyme, but in July 1277 Edward I, who was then at Eccleshall, sent them 6s 8d for one day's food. Since the king customarily gave fourpence per friar, there may have been twenty in residence at that time. In 1291 Queen Eleanor of Castile left them 100s, and when staying at the castle in Newcastle, Edward II sent them 4s.

During the 1350s, Henry, Duke of Lancaster, released them from the need to pay rent to him for their house, and allowed them to expand into neighbouring buildings. It seems that this community had been simply renting existing premises, and lacked any founding endowment.

Another unique feature of the Staffordshire Dominicans is their closeness to the original spirit of their order. At the end of the fourteenth century a dispute arose over how rigorously to follow the original ideals of the founder. Many brothers were eating and sleeping in their own private rooms, and providing themselves with their own furniture, books, clothing and food. Charles Palmer describes their state as one of leading private lives within their communities. This was resisted by a conservative minority, who felt compelled to maintain a fully common life. In 1390 the Master-General appointed William of Barleton to gather into the house at Newcastle-under-Lyme all those friars who rejected the various compromises and relaxations which had been commonly adopted, and who wished to cling rigorously to the founder's original aims.

In 1471 the provincial chapter of the Order is known to have met at Newcastle, although it probably did on other occasions as well. Yet in the sixteenth century, the bishop of Dover found the priory 'all in ruin and a poor house, the choir lead and the cloister lead ready to fall down, the rest slate and shingle'. The friars owed various people over fourteen pounds so that 'all their substance lay in pledge, and yet all not worth the debt; so that no store was in the house but all gone'.

The Augustinian Priors

A number of congregations of hermits in central and northern Italy who had been following the Rule of St. Augustine were grouped together and established as a order, known as the of Augustinian Hermits, by Pope Innocent IV in 1244. In 1256, Pope Alexander IV called them to active work in the cities, where they became known as the Austin Friars (not to be confused with the Austin canons). The order spread rapidly throughout Europe, and they took a prominent part in university life and ecclesiastical affairs.

Stafford Austin Priory

In 1343, Ralph, Lord Stafford, petitioned the pope for permission to found a house of Austin friars in Forebridge, a suburb to the south of Stafford. The Pope gave permission, provided that the endowment should be sufficient to support twelve friars, which was to be part of the order's administrative area of Ludlow. Lord Stafford provided five acres for the site, and his brother-in-law, Humphrey de Hastang, archdeacon of Coventry, donated a well from which an underground aqueduct could be built. A community was in residence by 1346.

The first prior, John of Wirksworth, was succeeded by two others in the same century with the same surname, suggesting that a single family probably had great influence and interest in the house. During the fourteenth century it may have been for some period one of the larger communities of the order, for in one year, 1320, no less than twenty-four men from this house were ordained. In 1403 King Henry IV stayed there after his victory at the battle of Shrewsbury.

Its later poverty is attested by the fact that at the dissolution the priory possessed only a minimal number of church furnishings and ornaments, and these were described as 'very worn'. There were no jewels, a single chalice, and 'one little wooden cross plated over very thin with silver'.

Linda Owen

Tomb of Sir John Gifford of Chillington, in Brewood Parish Church.

Linda Owen

The Fulgehame Monument in Checkley Parish Church. Geoffrey Fulgehame purchased the site of Croxden Abbey in 1544. According to a local tradition recorded by Sister Mary Lawrence, he was reconciled to the Catholic Church when he made his dying confession to one of the former monks then living with the Rector of Draycott. A worn alabaster slab beside this monument marks the tomb of Geoffrey Chawner (Chalnar), last abbot of Croxden. The inscription, now illegible, records his burial on 30th April 1544.

chapter seven
the dissolution

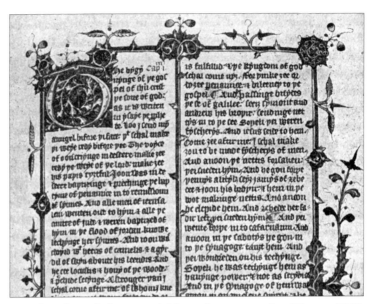

Their were strong movements against the power and wealth of the church through the 14th, 15th and 16th centuries leading up to the actions of Henry VIII. John Wycliffe (1320-1384) was the most famous critic of the Pope and his power in England. This is part of the first page of the gospel according to St Mark in Wycliffe's first translation of the bible into English.

All the religious houses were to be closed down within a few years by Henry VIII. Although in retrospect this seems a dramatic development, the dissolution of the monasteries was not entirely without precedent. The Templars had been banned in order to seize their assets, while the alien houses had been systematically attacked during the Hundred Years War with France. During the years immediately before the Dissolution, several further precedents were to be established for what was to follow.

By the sixteenth century the fashion among the very rich was to endow colleges at the universities of Oxford and Cambridge. In 1524 Cardinal Wolsey decided to close twenty-one poor religious houses in order to endow a new college at Oxford, to be known as Cardinal College. The list drawn up included Canwell and Sandwell Priories. At that time both houses were in a ruinous condition. At Canwell, the timber was in a bad state, and all but one side of the cloisters had fallen down. Each had a prior and only one other monk, and these agreed to hand over their estates and find themselves places in other houses of their order.

While he was in Staffordshire in 1526, Wolsey visited Lichfield, and apparently as a consequence of this visit, in the next year he also dissolved Farewell Priory. The income from its estates was to go to the support of the Cathedral choristers, replacing a payment due to the Chapter from Wolsley's new college. By the end of April of that year, the sisters had all been dispersed to other nunneries.

In 1530 the prior of Calwich died, leaving a single canon in residence. Although the bishop normally nominated a prior, Sir Ralph Longford decided to insist upon his right as patron to choose a successor. Investigation into the bishops' registers showed that if this right had ever existed, it had been in abeyance for at least two hundred years. But having had their attention drawn to another community which had virtually expired, the authorities decided to close it down. In April 1532 an agreement was drawn up by which Lord Longford would pay a rent for the estate. In March 1533, the goods of the priory were sold off, and the remaining canon sent to another house of the order. This procedure, leasing the estates of a religious house to a local landowner in return for a rent, clearly foreshadowed what was to come.

The early 1530s saw a series of acts of legislation designed to anglicise the Church in England. In 1533, appeals to the papal court were forbidden, and in the next year the payment of taxes to Rome was prohibited. In that year also, English monks were forbidden to travel abroad. All licences and dispensations were henceforth to be obtained from the English government rather than from Rome. Finally, with a few exceptions, all the English monks, friars and nuns swore the Oath of Allegiance signifying their acceptance of the king of England as supreme Governor of the Church in England. In so doing, they placed themselves at the mercy of the king's ministers.

In January 1535 Thomas Cromwell was given authority to act for the King in all ecclesiastical matters. The significance of this move seems to have been immediately apparent to some heads of religious houses.

Thomas Whitney of Dieulacres had already begun leasing the abbey lands to his relations in 1534, when John Whitney received a seventy-year lease of Swythamley Grange. In April 1536, Nicholas Whitney was given a lease of Rossall Grange for sixty years. In 1537 Humphrey Whitney received the salt-pit in Middlewich, and Geoffrey Whitney a pension from the manor of Leek.

In January 1535 Abbot Edward Wilkins leased Hulton's Rushton Grange, in Cobridge, for forty years to Richard Wilkins and Richard Barton for the generous rent of £4 per annum.

In February, Abbot Thomas Chawner of Croxden made out two deeds for sixty years for a farm called the Grange in Crakemarsh and land in Combridge to Geoffrey Chawner for the very low rent of £2 per annum. Mary Lawrence considered the purpose of this transaction to be to 'see that generation of Chawners into their graves'.

Ominously, a survey was made of the wealth of the religious houses, followed by a special visitation of the monasteries by the king's commissioners. Its purpose was to provide the evidence which would justify the dissolution of those religious communities whose way of life was considered unsatisfactory. Following scrutiny of the results of the visitation, legislation was presented to Parliament for the conversion 'to better uses' of all houses with an annual income of less that £200 on 11th March, 1536. All the religious houses in the area we have covered, except Burton, Lilleshall, Tutbury, Dieulacres and St. Thomas's Priory, Stafford, were covered by the terms of this act.

With the creation of the Court of Augmentations to administer the confiscated properties on behalf of the Crown, local commissioners were appointed to manage the estates. There were no immediate expulsions: 'We have left the canons and monks still in their houses, without any clear discharge of them, but have put them at their liberty and choice whether they will abide there until the King's grace's pleasure be further known therein, or else go from thence to their friends......'.

An unseemly scramble for their lands and other possessions promptly began. Probably never in history did so many wealthy men pen so many piteous begging letters. George Touchet, heir of Henry of Audley, made an attempt to be considered favourably as beneficiary of the lands and property which his ancestors had originally donated to Hulton Abbey, while Lord Stafford put in a plea for Stone Priory. Bishop Rowland Lee asked for the home estate of St. Thomas's Priory, Stafford, on the rather dubious grounds that since the original grant of land had been made by a previous bishop, he ought to have 'preferment of the house and demesnes for one of my kinsfolk'.

Prior William Smyth of Stone was apparently quite unmoved by the trend of events. He had ordered some timber from the bishop for rebuilding work. The bishop, seeing the way matters were developing, delayed delivery. In February 1537 the prior wrote: 'If I have not the said timber, I know not where to be provided for my great work now in hand'.

In March Lord Stafford wrote to Cromwell that the commissioners were expected at Stone on the following Sunday, but that the prior 'thinks his house shall stand; whereof the country is glad'. Lord Stafford evidently considered so too, for he promptly asked for Ranton Priory instead.

Both Sir Simon Harcourt and Henry, Lord Stafford, had made bids for this small estate. Harcourt managed to preserve some dignity: 'I beg you...... that the house may continue, and he shall have £100 and you £100 of you can accomplish it, and £20 fee out of the said house. If the king is determined to dissolve it I desire to have it as it adjoins such small lands as I have in the country, and I and my heirs will pay so much as the rent of assize cometh to and will give you 100 marks'. Stafford argued: 'it is within four miles of my house and reaches my park pale, and I will give as much for it as any man.....' A subsequent letter of his was merely pathetic: 'I have 12 children, and my living £40 a year less than it has been'.

Many communities were determined to survive, and number were allowed to continue on payment of a fine, technically as royal re-foundations. An attempt was evidently made at Stone to raise money to avert closure, for the prior mortgaged a silver gilt shrine, probably that of Saint Wulfad. But much of the priory silver had been embezzled by this time, including four standing cups and two salt cellars. The priory was dissolved sometime during the spring of that year. Lord Stafford moved the alabaster tombs of members of his family from the priory church at Stone to the Austin friary at Stafford, showing that at that time he had not yet grasped that there was going to be a general dissolution of all the religious houses.

The choice of which houses should be allowed to continue may have been made according to the whim of the King or his officials, perhaps taking into account local conditions. Since at this time dispossessed religious were being given the opportunity, if they wished to do so, to move to another house of their order, it might have been inconvenient to close down all the houses of a particular order in a given area, as the promised alternative accommodation would then have been difficult to provide. F.A. Hibbert thought that the intervention of powerful allies at court also explains the survival of some of them.

The fines levied were usually set at a level close to the annual income of each house. It is hardly surprising, therefore, that some time was to elapse before the required amounts were raised and licences to continue the religious life obtained. Rocester, the first Staffordshire house to purchase exemption, received its licence as early as March 1537, Repton on 12 June, after paying the very heavy fine of £266 13s. 4d. Croxden paid in July, while Hulton, the last of the Staffordshire houses to do so, received its charter on October 1st.

Notwithstanding this settlement, towards the end of 1537 rumours began to spread that all the monasteries were to be closed. Although in March 1538 Cromwell wrote to all heads of religious houses, pointing out that all the surrenders had been voluntary, and that a general closure of monasteries was not contemplated, it was becoming clear that heads of communities who wished to be treated well would be well advised to consider voluntary surrender very seriously.

Something of the pressure put upon the monasteries at this time by local landowners may be inferred from a letter of Abbot Thomas Whitney of Dieulacres to Cromwell in April 1538: 'We have no more churches but one adjoining our monastery...... and no granges or demesne lands in our own hands; only a few closes to keep our horses and cattle. We beg therefore that such small things as we have may remain in our possession, for divers gentlemen make great labour to the King to have them from us'.

In May, Abbot John Massey of Combermere was summoned to London to surrender his house. He arrived with a letter from Bishop Rowland Lee praising his 'gentle entertainment of me and other members of the council [of the Marches]', and expressed the hope that, while he was prepared to give up his place as abbot, he and his brethren might continue their life at Combermere. It was not to be. The house was surrendered on 27th July.

Near the end of August, Abbot Edward Wilkins of Hulton received what must have been a not unexpected summons to a similar interview. There could have been little doubt about its significance. The lay associates of Hulton Abbey clearly understood the situation. A deed leasing Mixon Hay to Sir Philip Draycot, and another leasing Knypersley tithe barn to Richard Biddulph were signed and sealed. Draycot's deed was given to Biddulph and Biddulph's to Draycot on the understanding that if the house were not suppressed then each man was to return the deed in his possession to the abbot. If the house were suppressed, then the two would exchange their deeds so that each could establish claim to the property of his choice.

On 20th August an approach for the lands of Hulton Abbey was made on behalf of George Touchet by his father, who also appealed to the principle that the closest descendants of the original founder of a house should have the best claim to its property, 'because, by their great hypocrisy and dissimulation they have gotten of my ancestors much of their patrimony'. This was followed up by a letter from Sir Brian

Tuke, Treasurer of the King's Chamber, his father-in-law, who pleaded that his son-in-law and daughter had 'no manor house to dwell in but an old, ruinous castle [Heleigh], almost all fallen down...'

In four days in August, Richard Ingleworth, bishop of Dover, closed all the houses of the friars in Staffordshire. He was at Lichfield on 7th August. Writing to Cromwell he said that the warden of the Franciscan friary, Richard Mason, who was hideously disfigured in the face 'whether of a canker or a pock or a fistula I know not', was loath to give up the house, even though its debts were greater than the value of everything in it. On the 9th he was at Stafford, where he closed down the Franciscan and Austin friaries. On the next day he arrived at Newcastle-under-Lyme, where he received the surrender of the Dominican friary in the presence of the mayor, bailiffs and others.

In September the Staffordshire suppression commissioners resumed their work, receiving formal surrenders of those monasteries which had paid fines to be allowed to continue, together with those larger monasteries not covered by the previous act of Dissolution. They were to sell all moveables except lead and bells, to pay off the debts of the dissolved houses, and to assign pensions to the expelled religious.

No time was wasted. On the 14th Thomas Legh secured the closure of Tutbury Priory. The surrender of Rocester and Croxden followed on 17th September. On Monday 23rd September, he was at Hulton. At some time in October, the priory of St. Thomas, Stafford, was surrendered. On 16th October, Legh took the surrender of the Black Ladies Priory at Brewood and Lilleshall. On 20th he was at Dieulacres. The Priory of Repton was surrendered on 25th October.

One task of the commissioners was to take custody of the seals of the various communities, so that their lands and property could not be legally alienated. In the flamboyant style we should expect of the abbots of Dieulacres, Thomas Whitney had previously taken the precaution of making out a number of blank charters and affixing the abbey seal to them. These he then used to write back-dated leases to various associates, such as John Brereton.

Although Burton Abbey was spared, in 1538 Sir William Basset commandeered the famous statue of Saint Modwen, defaced its reliquary, and prohibited further offerings at the shrine. He sent the statue to Thomas Cromwell by his brother, Francis Basset, one of Archbishop Cranmer's servants. In November of that year the last of the Staffordshire houses, and also the oldest, was closed down when the abbot and monks of Burton surrendered to Dr Thomas Legh.

The officials of the Court of Augmentations moved quickly to appropriate the assets of the dissolved monasteries, presumably in order to anticipate and prevent looting by the monks, their officials and servants, or rapacious neighbours. John Scudamore, the Receiver-General for Staffordshire, had instructions to survey all the land and goods of the surrendered houses, to make returns of their annual value, to sell by auction all moveables at the conventual buildings, and to acquire for the Crown the lead from the church roofs. He passed through the county close behind the visitors.

The primary purposes of the enemies of the religious communities were to raise money for the Crown and to render the sites of the monasteries unusable for their original purposes in the future. Outside the towns this usually resulted in the immediate destruction of the church. The first step in this process was smashing the windows and removing the roofs.

Evidence of this initial process of destruction has been brought to light by excavations carried out on the site of Hulton Abbey, where a destruction level has been identified, characterised by small amounts of window lead and fragments of decorated window glass. The lead on the roofs was the property of the Crown. It was stripped off, melted down and cast into pigs, the roof timbers or wooden choir stalls often being used as fuel, although the choir stalls of Combermere were probably taken to Nantwich Parish Church, and those of Lilleshall to Wolverhampton.

Despite their speed, the royal officials were not always quick enough to prevent losses. Legh, wrote to Cromwell that when they arrived at Repton they found the house spoiled and many things removed, only some of which they were able to recover.

There is no evidence of active opposition to the dissolution in Staffordshire. The friars, however, seem to have been more popular than the monks. Richard Ingleworth, responsible for suppressing the friaries of North Wales and the West Midlands, complained that they 'have many favourers, and great labour is made for their continuance'. One reason for this may have been that as landowners they did not employ rent collectors.

The Dissolution of the monasteries would have occasioned a less traumatic break with the past than we sometimes imagine. Most houses contained few brothers, and most administration and working of estates was done by laymen. Many of the ejected monks moved their quarters a matter of yards rather than miles to take up residence with their families, who already enjoyed leases of abbey lands. For example, Abbot Thomas Whitney of Dieulacres took up residence in Mill Street, Leek. The monks were awarded pensions, although sometimes these were not paid regularly. In December 1540, Whitney wrote to the Court of Augmentations asking on behalf of himself and his 'poor brethren' to be paid the instalment due on the previous Michaelmas Day, and for the pensions to be paid on time in future. A recent study suggests that the Giffords may have allowed the nuns of the Black Ladies' Priory to live out the rest of their lives in the Priory buildings. They may have continued to function as a secret nunnery for some time.

A small minority of the religious were able to gain livings as churchmen. Prior Arthur Meverell of Tutbury became vicar in 1543, but resigned a year later to become vicar of Tideswell, in Derbyshire. Prior Whytell of St. Thomas, Stafford, became vicar of Audlem in 1539, retaining this post until his death eighteen years later. The abbot and four of the monks at Burton became members of the College of Burton, which was formally founded in 1541, but which only lasted for four years. Others found useful employment in other ways. William Asshenhurst of Hulton seems to have taken up teaching at Stoke Church. It is known that many English friars, being used to greater mobility and having less to lose, left the country.

Most of the lands of the religious houses were purchased by local gentry. Some, such as Sir John Gifford of Chillington and Sir Edward Littleton of Pillaton Hall, purchased large numbers of estates from many different houses, some of which they immediately resold. Despite a certain amount of property speculation by rich Londoners, a century after the Dissolution of the monasteries most of the Staffordshire property they had purchased was firmly in the hands of the local gentry.

There is some indication of a lingering hope among some people that the suppression might only be temporary. In 1556 Margaret Sutton of Stafford left a bequest of cloth to one of the friaries in that town 'if it go up again'. Thomas Whitney, last abbot of Dieulacres, left provision in his will that a chalice from the abbey he still had in his possession be restored if it 'be hereafter edified'.

Most of the gentry had a stronger interest in ensuring that no such reverse should shake their fortunes. In 1548 Gilbert Thacker who inherited the Priory of Repton became alarmed at the news that Queen Mary had reopened Westminster Abbey. The antiquarian Fuller says: 'upon a Sunday (belike the better day, the better deed) [he] called together the carpenters and masons of that county, and plucked down in one day (church work is a cripple in going up, but rides post in coming down) a most beautiful church belonging thereto, saying he would destroy the nest, for fear the birds should build therein again'.

The strength of the attachment of the few remaining Catholics to some of these sites is demonstrated by their use of the White Ladies Priory at Brewood as a burial place until 1844.

A scene from the Stoke Historical Pageant and Wedgwood Bicentenary Celebrations held in Hanley Park in May 1930. In this episode people of the Potteries depict the sale of the effects, goods and chattels of Hulton Abbey.

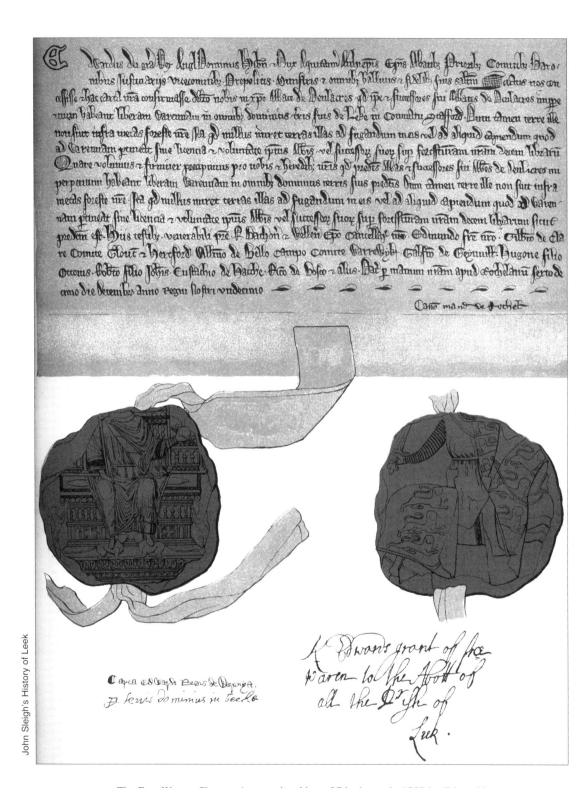

The Free Warren Charter given to the abbot of Dieulacres in 1283 by Edward I.

chapter eight
the sources

History is mainly the product of the work of historians in assessing the significance of ancient documents. Perhaps the most obviously useful in this context is the monastic chronicle. These are records of significant events, sometimes made at the time they occurred. They vary in usefulness, depending upon the interests of those who made them. Some are brief, while others are very informative. Some are preoccupied with local matters, while others deal with national events.

At Burton Abbey a chronicle known as the *Annals* was kept from the foundation of the Abbey in 1004 until 1262. It has proved particularly useful to students of the political history of England during the thirteenth century. A chronicle of Dieulacres in the Gray's Inn Library, London, is of considerable importance to scholars in establishing events during the reign of King Richard II, and his deposition at the end of the fourteenth century.

The *Croxden Chronicle* in the British Museum gives invaluable details about local weather and the crops. The Chronicler records the climate changes and other disasters during the early fourteenth century, which brought the initial period of prosperity of the religious houses to an end. For example, he records that in 1345 the autumn was very rainy, and during that winter most of the sheep and other animals perished from rot, famine and cold. The year 1349, the year that the Black Death arrived in Staffordshire, contains the terse entry: 'there was a great pestilence throughout the whole world'. There are no more entries until that of 1361, which reads: 'There was a second pestilence, and every child born since the first pestilence died'. In 1369 the chronicler records that the lay brothers' wing fell down. During 1370 a flood swept away all the bridges over the Churnet and ruined the grass in the water meadows. At the beginning of February a violent storm uprooted half the trees in the orchards, blew down two barns and damaged the roofs of the monks' dormitory, the abbot's house and the infirmary.

Charters and deeds record various legal transactions, such as the donation and leasing of lands. Monks and canons were usually extremely careful to preserve evidence of their legal rights to their lands, to services due to them and to privileges which they enjoyed, by making abbreviated summaries of all their important legal documents, called cartularies. A cartulary of Burton Abbey lies in the British Museum, a cartulary of Dieulacres is kept in the William Salt Library, Stafford, and a cartulary of Tutbury Priory lies in the College of Arms, in London.

There are many other kinds of documents which have sometimes survived. An account of the life and miracles of Saint Modwen, written by Abbot Geoffrey (1114-50) of Burton, in the British Museum, details over thirty miracles allegedly performed by the saint from the years immediately before the Norman Conquest to his own time. It is also quite informative of the history of the Abbey. Also in the British Museum is a register of the names of all the abbots and monks of Croxden. In the

The Potteries Museum

Above: Lead Papal bulla of Pope Innocent VI (1352-62), probably taken from a document issued to Hulton Abbey in 1354 authorising the appropriation of the income of Audley Church. It was found on the chest of a male skeleton buried in the chancel of Hulton Abbey where it had probably been placed as a charm.

Archeological finds at the Hulton Abbey site

Right: Skeleton wrapped in rushes. Analysis of pollen grains found in the plant material showed them to have come from cereals and plants found in open rather than wooded country.

Below: Gold ring set with a sapphire found on a skeleton in front of the high altar. Abbots sometimes wore such rings, but evidence indicating that the skeleton was of a female suggests this one belonged to a member of the patron's family.

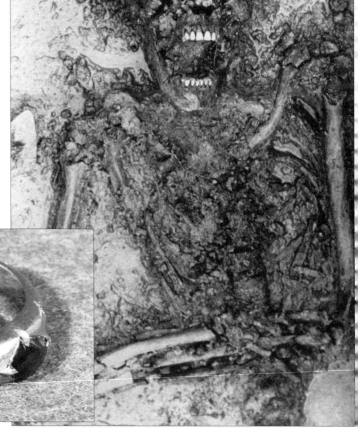

The Potteries Museum

An agreement between Abbot William of Hulton and Prior Roger of Trentham (1242) by which the canons of Trentham recognised the rights of the monks of Hulton to graze their sheep on Meir Heath, in return for which the monks ceded a disputed area of Lightwood Heath to Trentham Priory.
The agreement is in the form of an indenture. Two copies were written on the same piece of parchment and sealed. The parchment was then cut with a knife in an irregular fashion. If either party later contested the agreement the two pieces could be fitted together to prove the legally binding settlement both had agreed to.

records of the Land Registry in the Public Record Office is a rental of Hulton Abbey, a summary of rents due to the Abbey for lands and properties leased to tenants. A custumal, a detailed account of the rule of life observed, from the priory of Saint Thomas, lies in the library of Cambridge University. It is one of only three from English houses in existence.

Details about the history of the houses within our area may sometimes be gleaned from documents from others. Thus information about Calwich and Stone, originally daughter houses of Kenilworth, may be found in a cartulary of that priory in the British Museum. The *Letter Book* of Robert Joseph, a monk of Evesham Abbey, records his correspondence with Humphrey Chester, a monk of Combermere. Their letters were carried between the monasteries by a travelling fishmonger.

In addition to documents originally kept in the monasteries themselves, much can be learned about the medieval religious houses from the records of the government, the papacy, the religious orders and the diocese. Government records are kept in the Public Record Office in Chancery Lane, London. These include huge rolls of parchment containing abbreviated copies of all letters sent out by the royal government. There are also records of the royal courts, the Exchequer and the Court of Augmentations, set up to administer and dispose of the estates of the dissolved religious houses. Among the most important diocesan records, kept in the Lichfield Joint Record Office, are the bishops' registers and the records of the bishops' visitations of the monasteries. As we have seen, the latter give an informative insight into the state of affairs within the houses.

In addition to original documents, we sometimes have transcripts of documents, the originals of which have disappeared since they were copied. During the seventeenth and eighteenth centuries antiquaries such as Sir Peter Leycester, Sir William Dugdale and Thomas Loxdale copied many documents which have long since vanished. For example, the foundation charter of Rocester Abbey is now known only in transcript.

In dealing with what purport to be medieval documents, it is important to take account of the fact that people's interests have sometimes best been served by forgery. This is illustrated by two documents relating to Hulton Abbey. A set of supposedly medieval deeds was cut from a cartulary of Hulton Abbey and allegedly offered for sale to a member of the Sneyd family in the British Museum during the 1870s. These crude forgeries were almost certainly concocted at Keele Hall in order to provide the Sneyd family with support for their social pretensions by supplying them with a fabulous pedigree which would have connected their family to pre-Conquest English nobility

Even if the documents in question are genuinely medieval, it does not follow that they are necessarily reliable. A document purporting to be the Foundation Charter of Hulton Abbey, dated 1223, was kept at Trentham Hall until the eighteenth century, where it was copied by several distinguished antiquarians. It has since disappeared. This document traced the boundaries of the Abbey estates too widely, and mistakenly had Henry of Audley give the manor of Bradnop to the Abbey at its foundation. The original document by which that bequest was made, in memory of Earl Ranulph of Chester on his death in 1232, lies in the British Museum. The document kept at Trentham Hall was a sixteenth century forgery mentioned in a court case nearly fifty years after the Dissolution as drawn up by one of the last monks at the abbey, William Chawner, in order to justify a claim to lands of neighbouring estates.

Forgeries are by no means limited to legal documents. An engraving of the ruined interior of the church of Burton Abbey to be seen in the William Salt Library, Stafford, purportedly made in 1643 and so of great historical value, has been demonstrated by Ida Darlington to have been the product of a prolific forger during the mid-nineteenth century.

In addition to written records, historians are able to rely upon the work of archaeologists, who are able to use the material remains of the religious houses and of activities which have altered the landscape. Those houses most likely to suffer greatest destruction are those which were subsequently used as dwellings, since they have frequently been rebuilt several times, and those located in or near towns. Thus the material remains of the friaries are most liable to loss because, in addition to being less substantial to start with, they were all situated inside towns.

Paradoxically it is sometimes those sites which have suffered most damage from development which have been most investigated, since they lie in places of high population. Excavations have been conducted on the sites of Burton, Lilleshall, Croxden and Lichfield. However by far the closest attention has been paid to Hulton Abbey.

This is surprising as the site was damaged by the sinking of the foundations for a farmhouse through the chancel of the church in the middle of the nineteenth century, when local people played football with skulls which were dug up. Then in 1884, the landowner, the Rev. Walter Sneyd of Keele Hall, indulged in an amateurish and destructive dig, during which all moveable items of interest were sent to Keele Hall, many of which subsequently disappeared.

Yet during this century several careful, scientific excavations have been conducted on this site. Among the more remarkable artefacts uncovered are a gold ring set with an amethyst, a lead papal bulla of Pope Innocent VI (1352-62), and a pilgrim badge dating from the late fourteenth or early fifteenth century. Among the more remarkable burials of females was one containing two plaits of hair and a hazel staff, the mark of a pilgrim, and another which had uniquely been wrapped in rushes. Scientific investigation of these and other finds conducted by experts at the Potteries Museum has further extended our knowledge of the history of this house. For example, examination of the decay of the teeth of burials, probably of members of early patrons' families, shows evidence of the fine carbohydrate diet characteristic of the wealthy. Pollen analysis of grains found in the rush burial points to the cultivation of rye in open countryside. As scientific techniques develop, more information will be gleaned from what has already been uncovered, for example, using techniques of DNA analysis.

John Sleigh's History of Leek

An evocative artist's impression of a Dieulacres Abbey entrance,
Sleigh's *History of the Ancient Parish of Leek* 1883

chapter nine
in retrospect

From early times there seems to have been a genuine local tradition of hermits in and around Staffordshire, going back to the semi-mythical St. Bertelin, who is supposed to have lived on an island in the Trent where the town of Stafford later grew up, and spent the last years of his life at Ilam. Many monasteries were built on the site of hermitages, including Sandwell, Calwich, Radmore, Blithbury, Farewell, Yeaveley and probably Dieulacres.

The tradition of hermits did not die out with the coming of the monks, for in the twelfth and thirteenth centuries there were hermitages in Trentham, Ranton, Forton, Hamstall Ridware and Armitage. Most seem to have been in the woodlands, although some were situated in very public places. One may have been located by the bridge over the Dove at Tutbury, while another, cut into the rock near the road from Bridgenorth to Worfield, in Shropshire, enjoyed Crown patronage for some time. Paradoxically, later hermits seemed to have preferred human company, for they tended to live in towns and villages, such as Stafford, Wybunbury, Lichfield and Wolverhampton. There was an anchoress in Newcastle-under-Lyme in the early eleventh century.

Farewell and Radmore, and possibly Blithbury, originated as groups of hermits who had come to live together, between 1130 and 1150. This may indicate a mid-twelfth century local religious revival in the centre and south of the county. None established an independent order, the several communities adopting the rules of existing orders. All the other religious houses of medieval Staffordshire sprang from religious movements with origins outside the country, and in almost all cases, the movement would reach Staffordshire only after initial enthusiasm had begun to fade.

Even so, the twelfth and thirteenth centuries formed a period of intensive activity, with the erection of buildings and the organisation and exploitation of estates. It was during this period that much of the clearing of waste and development of estates was accomplished, in the case of the Cistercians, using the labour of lay brothers recruited locally. These advances were made under what were sometimes difficult conditions and in spite of breakdowns of law and order, particularly during the Barons' Wars of the 1260s and 1270s.

During the early years of the fourteenth century, there was a protracted crisis in the fortunes of most communities. This probably had several contributory causes. In a few cases the founding endowments were insufficient to sustain the size of the communities which had initially taken up residence. Absentee, hostile, and minority patrons may have left houses without effective lay protection during troubled times. Most important, the severe climate changes and epidemics among the livestock recorded in the Croxden Chronicle must have exacerbated the effects of other problems. These strains, and perhaps others of which we are ignorant, seem to have affected the internal cohesion of many communities, leading to a breakdown of authority and to considerable mayhem and violence. The coming of the Black Death in 1349 was the climax of these misfortunes, and many houses never recovered their numbers. During most of the fourteenth century many communities remained in desperate trouble and, frequently deeply in debt.

During the fifteenth century, when unfortunately records are comparatively scarce, it seems that some communities had achieved a degree of equilibrium. We see renewed initiative, and a willingness to engage in commercial enterprise. One or two houses actually prospered. But not all the religious communities enjoyed this recovery, and some continued to lurch from crisis to crisis. Ironically, by the beginning of the sixteenth century most had clearly recovered their numbers, stability and discipline. The few that had not either became a byword for crime and disorder, such as Combermere and Dieulacres, or ceased to function effectively as communities altogether, either because of internal dissensions, as at Stone, or low numbers, as at Canwell, Sandwell and Calwich. The houses of friars seem to have gone into catastrophic decline by the early sixteenth century.

Each order arrived after the initial enthusiasm of the founders had begun to dissipate. Apart from the ten year presence of Cistercians at Radmore, this strictest of orders was represented only by houses which had their origins in the problematic order of Savigny, which showed a cavalier disregard for the rules of their own order from the very beginning. Two of their abbeys were founded after new foundations had been forbidden, and within the prohibited distance from a sister house, and all were almost immediately raising money in ways which were specifically forbidden to them by the regulations of their own order.

Only the deliberate concentration of strict Dominicans at Newcastle-under-Lyme would have brought to the area something of the spirit of the founders, and that seems not to have been a success in the long term.

Hidden behind the barrier of the Pennines, the Staffordshire religious foundations were very distant in place and spirit of from their origins in the religious revivals on the mainland of Europe. Yet the establishment of the various orders here created for a few centuries a society more closely integrated with the rest of Western Europe than at any time until today. Many of the most influential people in the area belonged to organisations which, however loosely knit together, and however inefficiently managed, looked to what is now France, Italy, or even further afield, for the source of their inspiration and leadership. No language barrier existed because of the common knowledge of Latin and widespread use of French.

However much of a backwater Staffordshire may have been: whatever the physical difficulties attendant upon travelling abroad, whatever prejudices and resentments may have been generated by wars and by what may at times have appeared as high-handed interference in local concerns, the men of Staffordshire were deeply influenced by affairs on the continent of Europe. The produce of Lapley and Tutbury benefited monasteries in France. Events at Combermere, Croxden, Leek and Hulton were of concern to Chapters-General at Citeaux. The income from Keele and Yeaveley helped support knights fighting the Saracens in the Holy Land. In later years, the well-being of these estates would have been regularly noted by the authorities on the distant island of Rhodes. Affairs in Stafford and Lichfield would have been reviewed in Assisi. At the same time, all serious problems and disputes would ultimately have reached Rome. With the decline into aggressive provincialism during the late fifteenth and early sixteenth centuries, the fate of the multi-national religious orders in England, as well as that of the multi-national church, was sealed.

Despite their well-attested poverty, most of the religious communities of Staffordshire display those curious paradoxes which the historian R. W. Southern noted in connection with the Cistercians. Professing lives of poverty the monks and canons quickly built for themselves the most substantial (excepting only several castles) and comfortable (including the castles) living quarters for many miles around. They installed themselves as directors of corporations wielding considerable economic power in the local community. Professing lives of humility they formed a managerial aristocracy. Supposedly turning away from the concerns and cares of this world, we find them developing enterprises for profit, securing exemptions from tolls, resorting to law to preserve or extend their possessions, and engaging vigorously in local politics, (which, in and around Leek, usually seemed to involve maintaining large bands of armed men to intimidate opponents and tenants alike).

It should be borne in mind that despite their much advertised asceticism, the standard of living of the monks, canons and nuns, although probably not that of the friars, was considerably higher than that of the ordinary people of their day. The main difference would be between those forbidden to eat meat who sometimes did, and those allowed to meat any time they chose, but who could not afford to do so. In order to maintain realism it is necessary to compare the endowments of the houses with the numbers of religious men they contained, not to mention the bodies of servants they maintained. At the Dissolution the very modest community at Hulton was described as 'poor' and its buildings 'in a ruinous condition'. Yet we should remember that nine men, all sworn to a life of asceticism and domiciled in a single household, enjoyed the income of five manors and three parish churches. At the dissolution there were twenty one servants to eleven canons at Repton, eight servants to four nuns at the Black Ladies Priory, Brewood, and at Dieulacres thirty servants to thirteen monks. Most notable, is the ratio of twenty-nine servants to six canons at the Priory of Saint Thomas, Stafford.

It is clear that the rules of life of the various orders were never descriptions of the way those professing them actually lived, but rather ideals rarely, if ever, attained. At the basis of any rule was the regular round of worship and the common life. Any semblance of maintaining the regular round of monastic worship had at times fallen into total abeyance at Burton and Stone. There is evidence that by the sixteenth century the Cistercians of Croxden had given up holding the midnight office. It seems hardly likely that the considerably less well-governed monks of Combermere, Dieulacres and Hulton were persevering in it. Attendance at divine worship at any time of day at Repton was confined to a small minority of canons. Most heads of houses had their own private accommodation, with their own kitchens, and if the frequent references to hunting dogs in bishops' visitations are to be credited, they lived very much like country gentlemen. For most of the Staffordshire monks, by the sixteenth century both sleeping in shared dormitories and engaging in manual labour, and even such administrative duties as the supervision of workmen and the collection of rents, were inconveniences of the distant past.

The greatest material achievement of the monasteries during the Middle Ages, particularly of the Cistercians, is usually reckoned to have been the development of marginal lands by a unique combination of unified management and efficient organisation. But in order to evaluate this claim we need to bear in mind that over those years development took place throughout the region. The manors under monastic control would have been developed even if they had remained in lay hands, and the records do not indicate that manors under lay control lagged behind those in monastic hands. In respect of industrial development and commercial prosperity some lay manors were the scene of forward-looking enterprise well before the sixteenth century.

Most of the development of the marginal land on the monastic estates was in fact accomplished by laymen. The clearances managed directly by the Cistercian monasteries occurred during the early years when they had, in their lay brothers, a disciplined, unpaid labour force of locally recruited men. When they realised that they could obtain an income with less trouble by leasing land for money rents, and hiring and firing labour as and when required, they quickly got rid of the lay brothers. Much of the clearance of waste on the monastic estates was in any case accomplished by tenants. Thus the development on the manor of Bradnop, on the Hulton estate, was actually carried out by lay tenants expanding their holdings into the waste on Morridge, and paying the Abbey for the privilege.

The religious houses were, in fact, extremely inefficient enterprises. While they sometimes suffered from the attentions of hostile neighbours and unfair burdens imposed by royal patrons, their financial problems seem usually to have been a result of monumentally incompetent management, very often recognised as such at the time. Many heads of religious communities seemed to consider their promotion chiefly as an opportunity to enrich themselves, their families and their friends at the expense of the endowments of their house.

The standard, romantic, image of a monastic establishment which tends to colour our perception of the medieval scene hardly applied to Staffordshire at all after the end of the thirteenth century. Communities were usually very small by national standards, and became increasingly integrated into the secular world. By the fifteenth century rents were collected by lay bailiffs from hereditary tenants. The bailiffs would have supervised the work of hired labourers on the remaining lands not leased out, and held the manor courts. Laymen lodged permanently within monasteries as corrodians and servants. Servants of the patrons used the religious houses as convenient hostels. Many of the monks were members of families who were tenants of their communities, and many of the families of religious men held leases of abbey and priory lands, suggesting considerable blurring of community and family interests. During the greater period of their existence there would have been little to distinguish the religious manors from secular estates except the style of the buildings, and the dress and title of their proprietors.

Appendix One
Glossary of Religious, Legal and Architectural Terms

Many of the terms below have several overlapping meanings. I have included only those used in the text:

Abbey: a religious house of some status, headed by an abbot or abbess.

Abbot: head of a community of monks having some significant status.

Aisle: part of a church built on either side of the nave or chancel.

Alien house: a religious house founded by a French monastery as a dependency. Most did not contain a community living a common religious life, but were administered to raise money to support the mother house in France.

Anchoress: a female hermit.

Apse: a semi-circular end wall built onto the east end of a church, sometimes with radiating side chapels.

Bulla: a seal attached to a papal edict, or the document itself.

Canon: a man living in holy orders under a religious rule, (also a priest attached to a cathedral).

Cartulary: a document (book or roll) reproducing in abbreviated form the legal records of a monastery.

Cellarer: the monk appointed to supervise the material life of an abbey or priory. He was in charge of the lay brothers, the hired workers and the granges.

Chancel: the eastern part of a church, containing the main or high altar and the benches for those singing the service.

Chantry: an endowment or chapel for masses to be said for a special intention, usually for the dead.

Chapter: the corporation, or collective body, of canons attached to a cathedral, or of canons or monks attached to a religious house.

Chapter House: the place designed for meetings of the whole body of canons or monks in a cathedral or monastery, in which they would conduct their official business

Choir: the western area of the chancel, usually reserved for those singing the services. In a monastic church, this would be the monks.

Chronicle: a year by year account of events, local or national, sometimes written as they happened.

Compline: the last office of the day before retiring to bed.

Convent: a community of monks or nuns, or the dwelling in which they live.

Corrodian: a layman who was entitled to board and lodging in a religious house in return for the down payment of a lump sum of money.

County Palatine: the county of Cheshire (then including Lancashire) within which the earls of Chester had special rights giving them great powers of government and making them almost independent of the king.

Crypt: an underground room beneath a church, usually used for burials.

Demesne land: the land, usually near to the monastic buildings, cultivated directly by the monastery, and not leased out to others.

Diocese: the area under the jurisdiction of a bishop. Staffordshire and its surrounding borderlands lay within the diocese of Lichfield, although the bishop was sometimes attached to Coventry and occasionally to Chester, which all lay within the same diocese.

Dissolution: the closure of the monasteries.

Dormitory: the common room designated for sleeping.

Episcopal: of or to do with a bishop.

Excommunication: the process of ritually cutting a person off from the sacraments of the church, and from communication with other members of the church, a process accompanied by a solemn cursing. This was performed ceremonially by 'bell, book and candle' in the case of 'greater excommunication'.

Forest: a legally defined area, usually of wasteland, although not necessarily woodland, within which special forest laws were enforced.

Friar: a member of a fraternity living under a rule of life, but unlike monks, one not confined largely or entirely to a religious enclosure.

Friary: a house of friars.

Grange: an outlying farm of a Cistercian monastery, originally staffed by lay brothers. Later, an outlying farm of any religious house.

Habit: the distinctive dress of the members of a religious order.

Hermit: someone who has 'withdrawn from the world' and lives in solitude in order to devote himself to God.

Interdict: This was a solemn ban on the performance of any religious rites, including baptisms, masses & the blessings of marriage and funerals.

Lay brother: someone who has taken the vows and habit of a religious order, but does not intend to become a priest; employed chiefly in manual labour.

Marcher lords: nobles given compact estates in border areas by William the Conqueror in order to be able to resist incursions, e.g. the earls of Chester, Shrewsbury, Montgomery, Hereford and Gloucester.

Marches: borderlands. Cheshire, Shropshire, Herefordshire and Gloucestershire made up the Welsh Marches.

Mark: thirteen shillings and four pence.

Mass: celebration of the Eucharist or Lord's Supper.

Matins: the monastic office properly sung at midnight.

Misericord: an elaborately carved projection underneath hinged seats in a choir stall which, when the seat was turned up, would serve to support a person while standing.

Monastery: a religious house of monks.

Monk: a member of a community of men living under religious vows apart from the world, i.e. within the walls of a religious enclosure.

Nave: the western part of a church, where lay people stood.

Novice: a new member of a religious community, still under probation.

Nun: a member of a community of women living under religious vows apart from the world, i.e. within the walls of a religious enclosure.
Nunnery: a religious house of nuns.
Office: the regular daily worship of God offered in a monastery, usually offered eight times a day.
Parish: an area having its own church and clergymen.
Patrons: a powerful lay family, usually that of the founder, which acted as protectors, and usually benefactors, of a religious house.
Precincts: the area of a monastery enclosed by the boundary walls.
Prior: the second in command in an abbey, or the head of a smaller or subsidiary religious house.
Priory: a religious house headed by a prior.
Rectory: a benefice not appropriated by a religious house.
Refectory: the common room of a monastery designed for eating meals.
Religious house: a community of monks or nuns, or the dwelling in which they live.
Religious man: a man living under the rule of a religious order.
Religious order: a fraternity or religious men or women living according to a common rule of life.
Reliquary: a receptacle, usually made of precious metal, to contain the remains of a saint.
Rule: a code of discipline, defining a distinctive way of life, observed by a religious order.
Serfs: people legally tied to the land, so that they had to work the land they inherited and perform services or pay rent for it, or both, to their lord.
Sheriff: the chief officer of the Crown in a county, charged with keeping order, apprehending criminals, enforcing writs, etc.
Slype: a passage in the precincts of a cathedral or monastery, usually used for a passage from one of the transepts of the church to the chapter house.
Stalls: rows of long, carved wooden benches lining the walls of the choir.
Tithes: a tax, usually made in kind, of one tenth the produce of the land, payable to the church. This paid for the upkeep of the church building, provided an income for the priests who served the parish (the benefice). One third was supposed to be reserved as alms for the poor.
Transept: the transverse part of a cruciform church, set at right angles to the main axis of the building. Since the main axis of a church building lay west-east, the transepts can be distinguished as lying on the north or south sides.
Vicar: a representative of a religious community with the responsibility to serve the church.
Visitation: an inspection of a religious house, usually by the diocesan bishop or the father-abbot.
Writ: a legally authoritative written command issued in the name of the king or a court directing someone to act, or to abstain from acting, in some way.

Appendix Two
Bibliography

The starting point for all serious students of local history is the relevant volumes of the Victoria County Histories, available in large reference libraries:

Staffordshire: Una C. Hannam, M. W. Greenslade, A. Saltman, J. L. Kirby, A. P. Duggan, J. C. Dickinson, and Hilda Johnstone, *VCH Staffs, vol. 3.*

Cheshire: Ann J. Kettle, *VCH Cheshire, vol. 3.*

Derbyshire: J. C. Cox, *VCH Derbyshire, vol. 2.*

Shropshire: Marjorie M. Chibnall, *VCH Salop, vol. 2.*

General studies of Staffordshire monasticism:

Hibbert, F. A., *Monasticism in Staffordshire,* (Stafford, 1909)
Hibbert, F. A., *Dissolution of the Monasteries*, (London, 1910)

Detailed studies of aspects of the history of particular religious houses:

Burton: Bartlett, Robert, 'The Miracles of Saint Modwena of Burton', *Staffordshire Studies, 8* (1996) 24-35.

Dieulacres: Fisher, Michael J., *Dieulacres Abbey: Leek, Staffordshire*, (n.p., 1984)

Calwich: Fortescue, M. T., *History of Calwich*, (London & Winchester)

Croxden: Hibbert, F. A., 'Croxden Abbey', *Church Quarterly Review 75* (1912-13), 38-71.
Lawrence, M., 'St Mary's Abbey Croxden, Staffordshire', *Transactions of the North Staffs Field Club, LXXXV* (1951) to *LXXXVIII* (1954)

Stafford, Saint Thomas:
Lambert, Lionel, 'The Black Canons of Stafford', *Transactions of the North Staffs Field Club*, (1879).

Newcastle-under-Lyme:
Palmer, C. F. R., 'The Friar-Preachers of Newcastle-under-Lyme', *Reliquary 17* (1876) 130-4.

Keele: Studd, Robin, 'A Templar Colony in North Staffordshire: Keele Before the Sneyds', *North Staffs Journal of Field Studies, 22* (1982) 5-21.
Studd, Robin, 'From Preceptor to Prisoner of the Church: Ralph Taret of Keele and the Last of the Templars', *Staffordshire Studies, 8*, 36-49

Hulton: Tomkinson, John L., 'The Documentation of Hulton Abbey: Two Cases of Forgery' *Staffordshire Studies, 6* (1994) 73-102.
Tomkinson, John L., A History of Hulton Abbey, *Staffordshire Archaeological Studies, New Series 10*, (1997)

Repton: Taylor, H. M., St. Wystan's Church, Repton, (n.p., 1989)

Stone:	Beresford, W., 'Stone Priory', *Transactions of the North Staffs Field Club*, (1881) 24-25.
Tutbury:	Moseley, Sir Oswald, *History of the Castle, Priory and Town of Tutbury, (1832)*

For those wishing to read original documents in translation, the main source is the publications of the Stafford Record Society known as Staffordshire Historical Collections. They are to be found at the William Salt Library, Stafford, and in all major reference libraries in the county.

Of general interest is:

'Bishop Geoffrey Blythe's Visitation, c. 1515-25', ed. Peter Heath, *SHC Fourth series 7*.

Transcriptions relating to particular houses include:

Brewood, Black Ladies:
'Charters and Records', ed. G. P. Mander, SHC (1939)

Burton: 'Burton Chronicle', *Annales Monastici*, ed. H. R. Ward, Rolls Series (1864-9) vol. 1, 183-500.
'Cartulary', ed. Gen. Wrottesley, *SHC VI*
'Charters and Muniments', ed. I. H. Jeayes & M. Deansley, *SHC* (1937)
'A Rental of the Borough of Burton, 1319', ed. D. G. Stuart, *SHC 4th series vol. 16* (1994) 1-52.
'Surveys, 12th Century', ed. C. G. O. Bridgeman, *SHC* (1916)

Combermere: 'The Book of the Abbots of Combermere, 1289-1538', *Lancashire & Cheshire Record Society Journal, 31.*

Dieulacres: 'Cartulary', Gen. Wrottesley, *SHC IX NS*

Ranton: 'Cartulary', Gen. Wrottesley, *SHC IV*

Stafford, Saint Thomas:
'Deeds', ed. F. P. Parker, *SHC VIII*

Stone: 'Cartulary', ed. Gen. Wrottesley, *SHC VI, i.*

Trentham: 'Deeds', ed. F. P. Parker, *SHC XI*

Tutbury: 'The Cartulary of Tutbury Priory', ed. Arrom Sutman, *SHC Fourth series 4.*

Note:

In the nineteenth century writers in the *Staffordshire Historical Collections* used the term 'cartulary' loosely for collections of transcripts of documents from or relating to religious houses, put together by themselves.

Appendix Three
Site Guide

Blithbury Priory: There is some doubt about the location of the site.

Brewood (Black Ladies) Priory:
> Situated south of the A5 near the Gaily roundabout, about two miles west of Brewood. The present building probably incorporates masonry, timber and other features from the latest period of the nunnery.

Brewood (White Ladies) Priory:
> There are ruins of a late Norman church. During the sixteenth century a timber-framed house stood on the site, probably incorporating parts of the prioress's house. To this King Charles II was briefly taken after losing the battle of Worcester in 1651, before famously finding refuge in an oak tree outside nearby Boscobel House. The site, about two miles south-west of Brewood, is accessed by the lane leading first to Boscobel House.

Burton Abbey:
> The main part of the monastery lay to the west of the River Trent, bounded on the east by High Street and Lichfield Street. The church stood on a site occupied in part by Market Place and in part by the eighteenth century church of Saint Modwen. The nave of the abbey church survived until destroyed by an explosion of gunpowder during the Civil War. The late nineteenth century market largely covers the area of the cloisters. The Abbey Inn incorporates part of the abbey infirmary. The abbey sanatorium at Shobnall, Sinai House, which was rebuilt during the fifteenth century, may be reached from the A38.

Calwich Priory:
> There are no significant remains to be seen. A house on the site, which may incorporate some abbey masonry, was extensively rebuilt during 1849-50.

Canwell Priory:
> The stables of Canwell Hall, since demolished, are said to have been erected on the site during the late eighteenth century. There are no visible remains.

Combermere Abbey:
> The site is located off the A525 Audlem to Whitchurch Road near its junction with the A530 Nantwich to Whitchurch road. Parts of the abbey buildings are incorporated into the present Combermere Hall, including the oak hammer-beam roof of the refectory. Inaccessible to the public.

Croxden Abbey:
> There are extensive landscaped remains on private ground south of the B5032 Cheadle to Rocester road. The ruins of the church have been bisected by the road. The monastic chapel-by-the-gate was used as a parish church until it was demolished in 1886. Excavation of the abbot's lodging and infirmary took place during 1908-9.

Dieulacres Abbey:
> Just outside Leek, off the A523 Leek Macclesfield road, on private land,

(Abbey Farm). The site was partially excavated in 1770, and again in 1818, much of the stonework being removed or used for the outbuildings of Abbey Farm. In the fabric of the farm itself (1612) is a medieval timber-framed gateway and other parts of the abbot's house, while outbuildings incorporate pieces of dressed stonework as decorative features.

Farewell Priory:
> Farewell lies west of the A51 north-west of Lichfield. The conventual church survived intact until it was rebuilt in 1740. The east end of the present church retains masonry from the conventual church.

Hulton Abbey:
> Although nothing was visible above ground level, the site, lying east of the A5009 in Abbey Hulton, Stoke-on-Trent, has been partially but intensively excavated. The finds are displayed in the Potteries Museum and Art Gallery, Broad Street, Hanley.

Keele Preceptory: There are no remains to be seen.

Lichfield Priory: There are no remains to be seen.

Lapley Priory:
> North of the A5 just west of Gailey roundabout, some of the original fabric of the church remains. The priory stood on the north side of the church, on a site today partly occupied by the Old Manor House.

Lilleshall Abbey:
> The site lies south-east of the A518 Newport-Wellington road. In 1643 the buildings were fortified and garrisoned by the royalist Sir Richard Leveson. Parliamentary forced besieged the house and battered down some of the buildings before they were surrendered. The site was excavated in 1860, and during 1962-3. There are extensive landscaped remains on private ground, but with public access at weekends. These ruins are undoubtedly the most extensive, evocative and beautiful of any in the area covered.

Newcastle-under-Lyme Priory:
> The priory lay on the Lyme Brook, east of the castle in the angle of Blackfriars Road and Goose Street, on the site of Smithfield Cattle Market. There are no remains to be seen.

Radmore Abbey: The site is unknown.

Ranton Priory:
> A fourteenth century western tower and part of the adjoining south wall of the church remain on the estate of the Earl of Lichfield, south of the B5405, east of Stafford. Access is from the A5013 at Great Bridgeford.

Repton Abbey:
> Repton lies on the B5008 north of Burton-on-Trent. Saint Wystan's Church preserves a connection with the Saxon abbey, in its parish church. The Saxon crypt was the burial place of many of the kings of Mercia, the original site of the shrine of Saint Wystan, and a pilgrimage centre until the

early eleventh century. When the stairs were floored in and the windows obscured from view by buildings erected by Repton School, the existence of the crypt was forgotten. It was rediscovered in 1779 when a workman digging for an internment fell into it though the floor of the chancel.

Repton Priory:
> The western range of the canon's quarters became the original home of Repton School in 1557. Other remains of the medieval priory are incorporated into existing buildings, and extensive footings of the medieval buildings are visible in the grounds of the school.

Rocester Abbey: There are no remains to be seen.

Sandwell Priory: There are no significant remains to be seen.

Stafford, Saint Thomas's Priory:
> The site lies on private land within the grounds of Priory Farm. The cellars of the farm are medieval, and there are some slight remains of the priory buildings.

Stafford, Augustinian Priory:
> The site stood on the Green and to the south-west in Forebridge. Today the Roman Catholic Church of Saint Austin stands on part of the site. There are no remains to be seen.

Stafford, Franciscan Priory:
> The site lay east of the road from Stafford to Stone at the junction of Browning Street. The buildings were demolished during the Civil War to create a clear area for defence outside the town walls.

Stone Priory:
> In a cellar of 'The Priory', in Lichfield Street, is a cellar with a rib-vaulted ceiling, believed possibly to be part of the chapter house. There are also traces of the monastic building in the gardens of this property.

Trentham Priory:
> Only a small part of the priory church remains, incorporated in fabric of the parish church, which was rebuilt in 1844. It lies west of the A34 north of the entrance to Trentham Gardens.

Tutbury Priory:
> The nave of the priory church still stands, reduced in size, immediately below the castle walls. The west front displays the earliest known use of alabaster in England.

Yeaveley and Barrow Preceptory:
> Yeaveley lies east of the A515 Ashbourne-Lichfield road. There are remains in the grounds and incorporated into the fabric of the manor house at Stydd. A small section of the wall of the church was re-erected in 1915, but with the inside and outside of the wall reversed.